Quick

GENERAL
KNOWLEDGE
2020

A Concise Book on India and The World
with Current Affairs & Who's Who

by

RPH Editorial Board

Ramesh Publishing House, New Delhi

Published by
O.P. Gupta *for* Ramesh Publishing House

Admin. Office
12-H, New Daryaganj Road, Opp. Officers' Mess,
New Delhi-110002 ☎ 23261567, 23275224, 23275124
E-mail: info@rameshpublishinghouse.com
Website: www.rameshpublishinghouse.com

Showroom
● Balaji Market, Nai Sarak, Delhi-6 ☎ 23253720, 23282525
● 4457, Nai Sarak, Delhi-6, ☎ 23918938

Book Code: R-1716

ISBN: 978-81-942336-3-3

HSN Code: 49011010

Contents

❏ **Who's Who & Current Affairs** --------------- 1-8

❏ **Indian History** --------------- 1-26

✦ **ANCIENT INDIA:** Pre-Historic India; Indus Valley Civilisation (2500-1750 BC); The Vedic Period; Jainism and Buddhism; Emergence of Mahajanapadas; Dynasties of Ancient India; Mauryan Empire; Sangam Age (300 B.C. To A.D. 300); Gupta Period; Pushyabhuti Dynasty (600 - 647 A.D.).

✦ **MEDIEVAL INDIA:** Arab Conquest of Sind; Sultanate Period Bahmani and Vijayanagar Kingdoms; Mughal Empire (1526-1707 AD); The Marathas; The Sikh.

✦ **MODERN INDIA:** The Advent of the Europeans; East India Company; Governor-Generals of Bengal; Governor-Generals of India; National Movement (1885-1947); Indian National Congress (1885); Socio-Religious Movements and Organisation.

✦ **ART AND CULTURE:** Music; Culture Centres; Sculpture.

❏ **Geography** --------------- 27-40

✦ **WORLD GEOGRAPHY:** The Universe; Landforms; Oceans.

✦ **INDIAN GEOGRAPHY:** Area and Location; Climate; Soils of India; Transport.

❏ **Indian Polity** --------------- 41-51

✦ Indian Constitution; The Preamble; Important Articles; President; Council of Minister; National Symbols.

❏ **Indian Economy** --------------- 52-61

✦ National Income; Population; Poverty; Agriculture; Industry; Labour; Economic Planning; Money and Banking; Public Finance.

(iv)

❏ **General Science** ---------------- 62-95

+ **PHYSICS:** Physical Quantities; Force and Motion; Work, Power and Energy; Density and relative density; Heat; Wave Motion; Light; Sound; Electricity; Magnetism; Atomic and Nuclear Physics.
+ **CHEMISTRY:** Atomic Structure; Oxidation and reduction; Acids, Bases and Salts; Metallurgy; Carbon and its Compounds.
+ **BIOLOGY:** Branches of Biology; Animals/Plants; Cell Theory; Food; Diseases; Parts of Plants; System of Human Body.
+ **SPACE RESEARCH:** Indian Satellites in Space.
+ **COMPUTER:** Functions; Parts; Terminology; Programming.

❏ **General Knowledge** ---------------- 96-128

First in the World; Superlatives (World); Capital & Currencies; Geographical Explorations/Discoveries; World Famous Official Documents; Animals (Largest and Biggest); National Monuments of Some Famous Countries; The Seven Wonders of the World; Intelligence Agencies of Some Prominent Countries; Important Symbols or Signs; Major Languages of the World and their Speakers; Famous Newspapers of the World; Important News Agencies of the World; Name of Parliaments of Some Countries; Largest and Smallest Countries (Top 5); Religions of the World; National Emblems of Important Countries; First in India; Superlatives (India); Books and Authors; Important Dates and Days of the Year; Abbreviations; Indian Defence; United Nations Organisations (UNO); National Awards; Other National Awards; International Awards; Highest Honours of Some Countries; Sports; Olympics; Commonwealth Games; Asian Games; World Cup Cricket; Hockey World Cup; Football world cup; Important Cups and Trophies; Sports Measurements; Stadiums and Places Associated with Sports; Some Important Results.

✦✦✦✦

Indian HISTORY

ANCIENT INDIA

PRE-HISTORIC INDIA

- The history of human settlements in India goes back to pre-historic times.
- The archaeological remains are found in different parts of India to reconstruct the history of this period.
- In India, the pre-historic period is divided into the Palaeolithic (Old Stone Age), Mesolithic (Middle Stone Age), Neolithic (New Stone Age) and the Metal Age.

PALAEOLITHIC OR OLD STONE AGE

- The Old Stone Age sites are widely found in various parts of the Indian subcontinent. These sites are generally located near water sources.
- Man invented fire by rubbing two pieces of flint. Man used leaves, barks of trees and skins of animals to cover his body.
- A few Old Stone Age paintings have also been found on rocks at Bhimbetka and other places.

MESOLITHIC OR MIDDLE STONE AGE

- The next stage of human life is called Mesolithic or Middle Stone Age, which falls roughly from 10000 B.C. to 6000 B.C.
- The hunting-gathering pattern of life continued during this period.

- The use of bow and arrow also began during this period. Also, there began a tendency to settle for longer periods in an area. Therefore, domestication of animals, horticulture and primitive cultivation started.

NEOLITHIC AGE OR NEW STONE AGE

- During this period, the *wheel was invented*. It was a turning point in the life of man.
- The chief characteristic features of the Neolithic culture are the practice of *agriculture, domestication of animals*, polishing of stone tools and the manufacture of pottery.
- Large urns were used as coffins for the burial of the dead.
- The people of Neolithic Age used clothes made of cotton and wool.

METAL AGE

- The Neolithic period is followed by Chalcolithic (copper-stone) period when copper and bronze came to be used.
- The Chalcolithic age is followed by Iron Age.
- In the Iron Age, ploughs and daggers were made of iron. It led to the overall development of mankind.

INDUS VALLEY CIVILISATION (2500-1750 BC)

- The earliest excavations in the Indus valley were done at Harappa in the West Punjab and Mohanjodaro in Sindh. Both places are now in Pakistan.

Important Sites

- The most important sites are Kot Diji in Sindh, Kalibangan in Rajasthan, Ropar in the Punjab, Banawali in Haryana, Lothal, Surkotada and Dhaulavira, all the three in Gujarat.
- Mohanjodaro is the largest of all the Indus cities and it is estimated to have spread over an area of 200 hectares.

☞ **Indus Valley Civilisation : An Objective Study**

Major Sites	Excavators	Year	River	Location	Important Findings
1. Harappa	D.R. Sahni	1921	Ravi	West Punjab (Pakistan)	Granaries, Virgin Goddess, Cemetery, Stone symbol of Lingam and Yoni
2. Mohenjodaro	R.D. Banerjee	1922	Indus	Sindh (Pakistan)	Great Bath, Great Granary, Assembly Hall, Proto-Shiva, Brick Kilns, Mesopotamian seals
3. Chanhudaro	N.G. Mazumdar	1931	Indus	Sindh (Pakistan)	Bronze toy cart, Inkpot, Lipstick, City without a citadel
4. Kalibangan	B.B. Lal & B.K. Thapar	1953	Ghaggar	Ganganagar (Rajasthan)	Decorated bricks, ploughed field surface, Firealtars
5. Lothal	S.R. Rao	1957	Bhogwa	Ahmedabad (Gujarat)	Dockyard, Rice husk, Fire altars, Double burial
6. Banawali	R.S. Bist	1973	Ghaggar	Hissar (Haryana)	Toy plough, Gridiron pattern of Town planning.
7. Dholavira	R.S. Bist	1990	Luni	Kutchh (Gujarat)	A Large well & a bath, A stadium
8. Surkotada	J. Joshi	1964	—	Gujarat	Bones of Horse, Pot burials

Salient Features of the Harappan Culture

- The Harappan Civilization was primarily Urban.
- Mohanjodaro and Harappa were the planned cities.
- The large-scale use of burnt bricks in almost all kinds of constructions are the

Great Bath at Mohanjodaro

- important characteristics of the Harappan culture.
- Another remarkable feature was the underground drainage system connecting all houses to the street drains which were covered by stone slabs or bricks.
- The most important public place of Mohanjodaro is the Great Bath measuring 39 feet length, 23 feet breadth and 8 feet depth.
- Agriculture was the most important occupation. In the fertile soils, farmers cultivated two crops a year. They were the first who had grown paddy.
- Wheat and barley were the main crops grown besides sesame, mustard and cotton.
- Animals like sheep, goats and buffalo were domesticated. The use of horse is not yet firmly established.
- Bronze and copper vessels are the outstanding examples of the Harappan metal craft.
- A large number of seals numbering more than 2000 have been discovered.

Social Life

Harappan Seal

- Jewelleries such as bangles, bracelets, fillets, girdles, anklets, ear-rings and finger rings were worn by women. These ornaments were made of gold, silver, copper, bronze and semi precious stones.
- Fishing was a regular occupation while hunting and bull fighting were other pastimes.
- Manufacture of terracotta (burnt clay) was a major industry of the people.
- Figures of animals such as sacred bull and dove were discovered. The figures of Mother Goddesses were used for religious purposes.

- Most of the inscriptions were engraved on seals. It is interesting to note that the Indus script has not yet been deciphered.

Harappan Script

- The Pipal tree was used as a religious symbol.
- The origin of the 'Swastika' symbol can be traced to the Harrapan Civilization.
- The chief male deity was Pasupati, (proto-Siva) represented in seals as sitting in a yogic posture with three faces and two horns.

THE VEDIC PERIOD

RIG VEDIC AGE (1500 - 1000 B.C.)

- The Early Vedic period is known from the *Rig Veda*.
- The Rig Veda refers to Saptasindhu or the land of seven rivers. This includes the five rivers of the Punjab, namely, Jhelum, Chenab, Ravi, Beas and Sutlej along with the Indus and Saraswathi.
- Historians view that the Aryans came from Central Asia. They entered India through the Khyber pass between 2000 B.C. and 1500 B.C. They first settled in seven places in the Punjab region which they called Sapta Sindhu. Slowly, they moved towards the Gangetic Valley.
- The Aryan Civilisation was a rural civilisation.

Vedic Literature

- The word 'Veda' is derived from the root 'vid', which means to know and signifies 'superior knowledge'.
- The Vedic literature consists of the four Vedas – Rig, Yajur, Sama and Atharva.
- The *Rig Veda* is the earliest of the four Vedas divided into 10 mandalas and it consists of 1028 hymns. The hymns were sung by *Hotri* in praise of various gods.

General Knowledge

- The *Yajur Veda* consists of various details of rules to be observed at the time of sacrifice. Its hymns were recited by *Adharvayus*.
- The *Sama Veda* is set to tune for the purpose of chanting during sacrifice. It is called the book of chants and the origins of Indian music are traced in it. Its hymns were recited by *Udgatri*.
- The *Atharva Veda* contains details of rituals.
- Besides the Vedas, there are other sacred works like the Brahmanas, the Aranyakas, the Upanishads, and the epics Ramayana and Mahabharata.

Political Organisation

- During this period, the kingdom was tribal in character. Each tribe formed a separate kingdom.
- The basic unit of political organisation was *kula* or family.
- The highest political unit was called *jana* or tribe.
- There were several tribal kingdoms during the Rig Vedic period such as Bharatas, Matsyas, Yadus and Purus. The head of the kingdom was called as *rajan* or king.
- There were two popular bodies called the *Sabha* and *Samiti*. The former seems to have been a council of elders and the latter, a general assembly of the entire people.

Social Life

- Family was the basis of the society.
- The head of the family was known as *grihapathi*.

Economic Condition

- The Rig Vedic Aryans were pastoral people and their main occupation was cattle rearing. Their wealth was estimated in terms of their cattle.
- Carpentry was another important profession.

RELIGION

- The important Rig Vedic gods were Prithvi (Earth), Agni (Fire), Vayu (Wind), Varuna (Rain) and Indra (Thunder).
- Indra was the most popular among them during the early Vedic period.
- There were also female gods like Aditi and Ushas. There were no temples and no idol worship during the early Vedic period.

☛ Rigvedic Rivers

River	Name in Rigveda
Indus	Sindhu
Jhelum	Vitasta
Chenab	Asikni
Ravi	Parushini
Beas	Vipasa
Sutlej	Sutudri
Gomati	Gomal
Saraswati	Sarasvati
Ghaggar	Prishadavati

LATER VEDIC PERIOD (1000–600 B.C.)

- This age is also called as the Epic Age because the two great epics the Ramayana and Mahabharata were written during this period.
- The Sama, Yajur, Atharva Vedas, Brahmanas, Aranyakas, Upanishads and the two epics are the sources of information for this period.

Political Organisation

- Larger kingdoms were formed during the later Vedic period.
- The king performed various rituals and sacrifices to strengthen his position. They include Rajasuya (consecration ceremony), Asvamedha (horse sacrifice) and Vajpeya (chariot race).
- Kingship became hereditary.
- Kings assumed titles like Ekrat, Samrat and Sarvabauma.

Economic Condition

- Iron was used extensively in this period and this enabled the people to clear forests and to bring more land under cultivation. Agriculture became the chief occupation.
- Taxes like Pali, Sulk and Bhaga were collected from the people.
- Wealth was calculated in terms of cows.

Social Life

- The four divisions of society (Brahmins, Kshatriyas, Vaisyas and Sudras) or the Varna system was thoroughly established during the Later Vedic period.
- The Ashrama system was formed to attain 4 purusharthas. They were *Dharma*, *Artha*, *Kama* and *Moksha*.

Religion

- Gods of the Early Vedic period like Indra and Agni lost their importance. Prajapathi (the creator), Vishnu (the protector) and Rudra (the destroyer) became prominent during the Later Vedic period.

JAINISM AND BUDDHISM

JAINISM

- Jainism originated in the 6th century B.C. It rejected Vedic religion and avoided its rituals.
- Founded by Rishabha Deva. Rishabha Deva was succeeded by 23 Thirthankaras (prophets). Mahavira was the 24th Thirthankara.

Vardhamana Mahavira (540-468 B.C.)

- Vardhamana was born in a village called Kundagrama near Vaishali in Bihar.
- His father was *Siddhartha*. He was the head of a famous Kshatriya clan.
- His mother was *Trisala*. She was a princess of the Lichchhavi clan. She was the sister of the ruler of Vaishali.

- Vardhamana was married to Yasoda, a princess. They had a daughter.
- At the age of 30, he left his home and family. He became an ascetic (monk). He wandered from place-to place in search of truth for 12 years.

- In the 13th year of his penance, he attained the highest spiritual knowledge called Kevalya Jnana. Thereafter, he was called Mahavira and Jina. His followers were called Jains and his religion Jainism.
- He died at the age of 72 in 468 B.C. at a place called Pavapuri near modern Rajgir.

Teachings of Jainism

- The three principles of Jainism, also known as Triratnas (three gems), are:
  1. right faith.
  2. right knowledge.
  3. right conduct.
- Mahavira preached his disciples to follow the five principles. They are:
  1. Ahimsa—not to injure any living beings
  2. Satya—to speak the truth
  3. Asteya—not to steal
  4. Tyag—not to own property
  5. Brahmacharia—to lead a virtuous life.

Spread of Jainism

- Mahavira preached his religion in Prakrit language which was the language of the masses.
- Chandragupta Maurya, Kharavela of Kalinga and the royal dynasties of south India such as the Gangas, the Kadambas, the Chalukyas and the Rashtrakutas patronised Jainism.

General Knowledge

- Jainism was divided into two sects after Vallabhi Council, namely *Svetambaras* (wearing white dresses) under Sthulbhadra and *Digambaras* (naked) under Bhadrabahu.
- The first Jain Council was convened at Pataliputra by Sthulabahu, the leader of the *Digambaras*, in the beginning of the 3rd century B.C.
- The second Jain Council was held at Valabhi in 5th century A.D. The final compilation of Jain literature called Twelve Angas was completed in this council.

BUDDHISM

Gautama Buddha (563-483 B.C.)

- Buddha's original name was *Siddhartha*.
- Siddhartha was born in the Lumbini Garden near Kapilavastu in Nepal. His father was Suddhodana. He was a Sakya chief of Kapilavastu. His mother, Mayadevi, died when Siddhartha was only seven days old. He was brought up by his step mother Mahaprajapati Gauthami.
- At the age of sixteen Siddhartha, married Yasodhara and gave birth to a son, Rahul.
- The sight of an old man, a diseased man, a corpse and an ascetic turned him away from worldly life. He left home at the age of twenty-nine in search of Truth.
- He wandered for seven years and at last, he sat under a bodhi tree at Bodh Gaya and did intense penance, after which he got Enlightenment (Nirvana) at the age of thirty-five. Since then, he became known as the Buddha or 'the Enlightened One'.
- Buddha delivered his first sermon at Sarnath near Banaras (now Varanasi).
- He died at the age of 80 in 483 B.C. at Kushinagar in Uttar Pradesh.

Teachings of Buddha

- The Four Noble Truths of Buddha are:
  1. The world is full of suffering.
  2. The cause of suffering is desire.
  3. If desires are get rid off, suffering can be removed.
  4. This can be done by following the Eightfold Path.
- The Eightfold Path consists of:
  1. Right Thought.
  2. Right Belief.
  3. Right Speech.
  4. Right Action.
  5. Right Living.
  6. Right Efforts.
  7. Right Knowledge.
  8. Right Meditation.

Buddhist Literature

- In Pali language.

Gautama Buddha

- Buddhist scriptures in Pali are commonly referred to as *Tripitakas, i.e.,* 'Three Baskets'.
- *Vinaya Pitaka:* Rules of discipline in Buddhist monasteries.
- *Sutta Pitaka:* Largest, contains collection of Buddha's sermons.
- *Abidhamma Pitaka:* Explanation of the philosophical principles of the Buddhist religion.

☞ Main Buddhist Councils

Buddhist Council	Time	Place	Chairman	Patron
First	483 BC	Rajagriha	Mahakashyapa	Ajatshatru
Second	383 BC	Vaishali	Sabakami	Kalashoka
Third	250 BC	Patliputra	Mogaliputta Tissa	Ashoka
Fourth	AD 72	Kundalvana	Vasumitra, Ashwaghosa	Kanishka

EMERGENCE OF MAHAJANAPADAS

- In the beginning of the 6th century B.C., the northern India consisted of a large number of independent kingdoms.
- The Buddhist literature Anguttara Nikaya gives a list of sixteen great kingdoms called 'Sixteen Mahajanapadas'.

☞ **The Mahajanapadas**

Mahajanapadas	Capital
1. Kashi	Varanasi
2. Kosala	Shravasti
3. Anga	Champanagri
4. Magadh	Girivraj or Rajgriha
5. Vajji	Vaishali
6. Malla	Kushinagar and Pavapuri
7. Chedi	Shuktimati
8. Vatsa	Kaushambi
9. Kuru	Hastinapur, Indraprastha and Isukara
10. Panchal	Ahichhatra and Kampilya
11. Matsya	Viratnagar
12. Surasen	Mathura
13. Asmaka	Paudanya
14. Avanti	Ujjaini
15. Gandhara	Taxila
16. Kamboj	Rajpur (Hatak)

DYNASTIES OF ANCIENT INDIA

HARYANKA DYNASTY

- Bimbisara was the founder of Haryanka Dynasty.
- He was a contemporary of both Vardhamana Mahavira and Gautama Buddha.

- During his rule, Darius I, the Achaemenian emperor, conquered the Indus Valley area.
- Ajatasatru imprisoned his father Bimbisara.
- The first Buddhist Council was convened by Ajatasatru at Rajgir.
- The immediate successor of Ajatasatru was Udayin.
- Udayin laid the foundation of the new capital at Pataliputra situated at the confluence of the two rivers, the Ganges and the Son.
- Shishunaga was the founder of Shishunaga dynasty.
- After Shishunaga, the mighty empire began to collapse. His successor was Kakavarman or Kalasoka. During his reign, the second Buddhist Council was held at Vaishali.
- Kalasoka was killed by the founder of the Nanda dynasty.

NANDAS

- The fame of Magadha scaled new heights under the Nanda dynasty.
- Mahapadmananda was the founder of Nanda rule in Magadha.
- The last Nanda ruler was Dhana Nanda. Alexander invaded India during his rule.

MAURYAN EMPIRE

CHANDRAGUPTA MAURYA (322–298 B.C.)

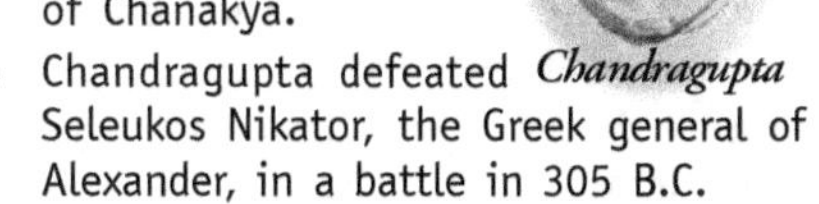

- Chandragupta Maurya was the founder of the Mauryan Empire. He overthrew Nanda dynasty with the help of Chanakya.
- Chandragupta defeated Seleukos Nikator, the Greek general of Alexander, in a battle in 305 B.C.

Chandragupta

- Seleukos sent Megasthenes as Greek Ambassador to the Court of Chandra-gupta. Megasthenes wrote *Indica*.

- Chandragupta was a follower of Jainism.
- He came to Sravana Belgola, near Mysore with a Jain monk called Bhadrabahu. The hill in which he lived until his death is called Chandragiri.
- Chanakya served as prime minister during the reigns of Chandragupta and Bindusara.

BINDUSARA (298–273 B.C.)

- Chandragupta Maurya was succeeded by his son Bindusara.
- Bindusara was called by the Greeks as *"Amitragatha"* meaning, slayer of enemies.

ASHOKA (273–232 B.C.)

- Ashoka was the most famous ruler of the Mauryan dynasty.
- The most important event of Ashoka's reign was his victorious war with Kalinga in 261 B.C.
- Ashoka convened the Third Buddhist Council at Pataliputra around 250 B.C. in order to strengthen the *Sangha*. It was presided over by Moggaliputta Tissa.
- Ashoka's edicts and inscriptions were deciphered by James Prinsep in 1837.
- The last Mauryan king, Brahadratha was killed by his minister Pushyamitra Sunga. It put an end to the Mauryan Empire.

SUNGAS

- The founder of the Sunga dynasty was *Pushyamitra Sunga*, who was the commander-in-chief under the Mauryas.
- He ascended the throne of Magadha in 185 B.C.
- Pushyamitra was a staunch follower of Brahmanism. He performed two asvamedha sacrifices.
- After the death of Pushyamitra, his son Agnimitra became the ruler.
- Agnimitra was a great conqueror. He was also the hero of the play Malavikagnimitram written by Kalidasa.

KANVA

- The last Sunga ruler was Devabhuti, who was murdered by his minister Vasudeva Kanva, the founder of the *Kanva dynasty*.
- The Kanva dynasty ruled for 45 years. After the fall of the Kanvas, the history of Magadha was a blank until the establishment of the Gupta dynasty.

SATAVAHANAS

- The founder of the Satavahana dynasty was Simuka.
- The greatest ruler of the Satavahana dynasty was *Gautamiputra Satakarni*.
- The greatest port of the Satavahanas was Kalyani on the west Deccan. Gandakasela and Ganjam on the east coast were the other important seaports.
- The fine painting at Amaravathi and Nagarjunakonda caves belong to this period.

SANGAM AGE (300 B.C. TO A.D. 300)

- The Sangam Age constitutes an important chapter in the history of South India.
- According to Tamil legends, there existed three Sangams (Academy of Tamil poets) in ancient Tamil Nadu popularly called Muchchangam. These Sangams flourished under the royal patronage of the Pandyas.
- *The first Sangam*, held at then Madurai, chaired by Agastya.
- *The second Sangam* was held at Kapadapuram, chaired by Tolkappiyar.
- *The third Sangam* at Madurai was founded by Mudathirumaran.

Political History

- The Tamil country was ruled by three dynasties namely the Chera, Chola and Pandyas during the Sangam Age.

CHERAS

- The Cheras ruled over parts of modern Kerala. Their capital was Vanji and their important seaports were Tondi and Musiris.
- The greatest Chera King was *Senguttuvan*.

CHOLAS

- The Chola kingdom of the Sangam period extended from modern Tiruchi district to southern Andhra Pradesh.
- Their capital was first located at Uraiyur and then shifted to Puhar. Kaveripattinam served as their port.

GUPTA PERIOD

- The Gupta period is considered as the *Golden Age* in the history of India because this period witnessed all round developments in Religion, Literature, Science, Art and Architecture.

CHANDRAGUPTA I (320-334 A.D.)

- In the beginning of the 4th Century A.D., Sri Gupta established a small Kingdom at Pataliputra. He is considered as the founder of the Gupta dynasty.
- The first notable ruler of the Gupta dynasty was Chandragupta I. He assumed the title *Maharajadhiraja*. The Meherauli Iron Pillar inscription mentions his extensive conquests.
- Chandragupta I is considered to be the founder of the Gupta era which starts with his accession in A.D. 320.

SAMUDRAGUPTA (335-380 A.D.)

- Samudragupta was the greatest of the rulers of the Gupta dynasty. The Allahabad Pillar inscription provides a detailed account of his reign.

Gold Coins of Samudragupta

- Because of his military achievements, Samudragupta was hailed as *'Indian Napoleon'*.

CHANDRAGUPTA II (380-414 A.D.)

- Samudragupta was succeeded by his son Chandragupta II Vikramaditya.
- The greatest of the military achievements of Chandragupta II was his war against the Saka *satraps* of western India.
- The famous Chinese pilgrim, Fahien visited India (A.D. 399 - A.D. 414) during the reign of Chandragupta II.

SUCCESSORS OF CHANDRAGUPTA II

- Kumaragupta (415-455) was the son and successor of Chandragupta II. His reign was marked by general peace and prosperity.
- Kumaragupta was the founder of the Nalanda University.
- Kumaragupta was followed by *Skandagupta* who ruled from A.D. 456 to A.D. 468.
- After Skandagupta's death, many of his successors like Purugupta, Narasimhagupta, Buddhagupta and Baladitya could not save the Gupta empire from the Huns. Ultimately, the Gupta power totally disappeared due to the Hun invasions and later by the rise of Yasodharman in Malwa.

PUSHYABHUTI DYNASTY (600 - 647 A.D.)

- The greatest king was *Harshavardhana*, son of Prabhakar Vardhana of Thaneshwar. He shifted the capital to *Kannauj*.
- *Hieun Tsang* visited during his reign.
- He established a large monastery at Nalanda. Banabhata adorned his court, wrote Harshacharita and Kadambari. Harsha himself wrote three plays— Priyadarshika, Ratnawali and Nagananda.

General Knowledge

PALLAVAS

- The Pallavas established their kingdom in Tondaimandalam by Simhavishnu with its capital at Kanchipuram.
- Other great Pallava rulers were Mahendravarman I, Narasimhavarman I, and Narasimhavarman II.
- The *Kailasanatha temple* at Kanchipuram is the greatest architectural masterpiece of the Pallava art.

CHALUKYAS (543-755 A.D.)

- Pulakesin I was the founder of the Chalukya dynasty. He established a small kingdom with Vatapi or Badami as its capital.
- The structural temples of the Chalukyas exist at Aihole, Badami and Pattadakal (Virupaksha temple). Cave temple architecture was also famous under the Chalukyas. Their cave temples are found in Ajanta, Ellora and Nasik.

RASHTRAKUTAS (755-975 A.D.)

- The art and architecture of the Rashtrakutas were found at Ellora and Elephanta.

CHOLAS

- Cholas became prominent in the ninth century and established an empire comprising the major portion of South India. Their capital was Tanjore.
- The founder of the Chola kingdom was Vijayalaya.
- Rajaraja Chola built the famous Brihadeeswara temple at Tanjore.
- *Dancing Figure of Shiva* (Nataraja) belong to Chola period.

MEDIEVAL INDIA

ARAB CONQUEST OF SIND

- In 712 A.D., Muhammad bin Quasim invaded Sind. Quasim defeated Dahir, the ruler of Sind and killed him in a well-contested battle.

Mahmud of Ghazni

- In 1024, Mahmud marched from Multan across Rajaputana, defeated the Solanki King Bhimadeva I, plundered Anhilwad and sacked the famous temple of Somanatha. This was his last campaign in India. Mahmud died in 1030 A.D.
- Mahmud patronized art and literature. *Firdausi* was the poet-laureate in the court of Mahmud.

Muhammad Ghori

- Prithviraj Chauhan defeated Ghori in the battle of Tarain near Delhi in 1191 A.D.
- In the Second Battle of Tarain in 1192, Muhammad Ghori thoroughly routed the army of Prithiviraj, who was captured and killed.
- After his brilliant victory over Prithviraj at Tarain, Muhammad Ghori returned to Ghazni leaving behind his favourite

general Qutb-ud-din Aibak to make further conquests in India.

SULTANATE PERIOD

SLAVE DYNASTY (1206-1290)

- The Slave dynasty was also called Mamluk dynasty. Mamluk was the Quranic term for slave.

Qutb-ud-din Aibak

- Qutb-ud-din Aibak was a slave of Muhammad Ghori, who made him the Governor of his Indian possessions.
- After the death of Ghori in 1206, Aibak declared his independence. He assumed the title Sultan and made Lahore his capital.
- Muslim writers call Aibak Lakh Baksh or giver of lakhs because he gave liberal donations to them.
- He built the famous Quwat-Ul-Islam mosque at Delhi. He began the construction of the famous Qutb Minar at Delhi but did not live long to complete it. It was later completed by Iltutmish.

Iltutmish (1210-1236 A.D.)

- Iltutmish belonged to the Ilbari tribe and hence his dynasty was named as Ilbari dynasty.
- He shifted his capital from Lahore to Delhi.
- He organised the *Iqta system* and introduced reforms in civil administration and army.

Raziya (1236-1240 A.D.)

- She appointed an Abyssinian slave Yakuth as Master of the Royal Horses.
- In 1240, Altunia, the governor of Bhatinda revolted against her. She went in personally to suppress the revolt but Altunia killed Yakuth and took Raziya prisoner.
- Bahram Shah, son of Iltutmish killed her.

Balban (1266-1286 A.D.)

- Balban introduced rigorous court discipline and new customs such as prostration and kissing the Sultan's feet to prove his superiority over the nobles.
- He also introduced the Persian festival of *Nauroz* to impress the nobles and people with his wealth and power.
- He established a separate military department - *diwan-i-arz* – and reorganized the army.

KHILJI DYNASTY (1290-1320 A.D.)

- The founder of the Khilji dynasty was Jalaluddin Khilji.
- Ala-ud-din Khilji was the greatest ruler of the Khilji Dynasty.
- He was the first Muslim ruler to extend his empire right upto Rameshwaram in the South.
- The Sultan had built a new city called Siri near Delhi.
- Amir Khusrau the great Persian poet, patronised by Balban, continued to live in Ala-ud-din Khilji's court also.
- He introduced the system of *dagh* (branding of horses) and prepared *huliya* (descriptive list of soldiers).
- Ala-ud-din Khilji maintained a large permanent standing army and paid them in cash from the royal treasury.

TUGHLAQ DYNASTY

- Ghiyas-ud-din Tughlaq was the founder of the Tughlaq dynasty.
- To have the capital at the centre of the empire and safe from the Mongol raids, Tughlaq chose Devagiri as his new capital in A.D. 1327. The Sultan renamed the new capital Daulatabad.
- In 1329-30, Muhammad-bin-Tughlaq introduced a token currency.
- Firoz Shah Tughlaq became Sultan after the death of Muhammad-bin-Tughlaq in A.D. 1351.

- He was the first Sultan to impose irrigation tax.
- He had built new towns of Firozabad, Jaunpur, Hissar and Firozpur.
- Timur Mongol leader of Central Asia, ordered general massacre in Delhi (AD 1398) at the time of Nasiruddin Mahmud (later Tughlaq king).

SAYYID DYNASTY

- Before his departure from India, Timur appointed Khizr Khan as governor of Multan. He captured Delhi and founded the Sayyid dynasty in 1414.
- Mubarak Shah, Mohammed Shah and Alam Shah were some of the other important noteworthy rulers of Sayyid Dynasty.

LODHI DYNASTY

- The Lodhis were Afghans.
- Bahlol Lodhi was the first Afghan ruler while his predecessors were all Turks. He died in 1489 and was succeeded by his son, Sikandar Lodhi.
- In 1504, Sikandar Lodhi founded the city of Agra and transferred his capital from Delhi to Agra.
- Babar marched against Delhi and defeated and killed Ibrahim Lodhi in the first battle of Panipat (1526).

BAHMANI AND VIJAYANAGAR KINGDOMS

- The break up of the Delhi Sultanate provided an opportunity for the rise of a number of kingdoms in the Deccan.
- After the decline of the Tughlaqs, there arose two important kingdoms in the Deccan. They were the Bahmani and Vijayanagar kingdoms.

VIJAYANAGAR EMPIRE

- The Vijayanagar Kingdom was set up in A.D. 1336. Its aim was to check the spread of Muslim power and protect Hindu Dharma in South India.

- Four dynasties – Sangama, Saluva, Tuluva and Aravidu – ruled Vijayanagar from A.D. 1336 to 1672.

Elephant Chariot – Hampi Ruins

- Vijayanagar was founded in 1336 by Harihara and Bukka of the Sangama dynasty.
- The Moroccan traveller, Ibn Batuta, Venetian traveller Nicolo de Conti, Persian traveller Abdur Razzak and the Portuguese traveller Domingo Paes were among them who left valuable accounts on the socio-economic conditions of the Vijayanagar Empire.
- The Hampi ruins and other monuments of Vijayanagar provide information on the cultural contributions of the Vijayanagar rulers.

KRISHNA DEVA RAYA (1509-1530)

- The Tuluva dynasty was founded by Vira Narasimha.
- The greatest of the Vijayanagar rulers, Krishna Deva Raya belonged to the Tuluva dynasty.
- Krishna Deva Raya himself authored a Telugu work, *Amukthamalyadha* and Sanskrit works, *Jambavati Kalyanam* and *Ushaparinayam*.
- He built the famous *Vittalaswamy* and *Hazara Ramaswamy* temples at Vijayanagar.
- Krishna Deva Raya renovated Virupaksha temple in A.D. 1510.
- After his death the enemies of Vijayanagar joined together and defeated the Vijayanagar ruler in the battle of Talaikota.

BAHMANI KINGDOM

- The founder of the Bahmani kingdom was Alauddin Bahman Shah also known as Hasan Gangu in 1347. Its capital was Gulbarga.

- Ahmad Wali Shah shifted the capital from Gulbarga to Bidar.
- *Gol Gumbaj* was built by *Muhammad Adil Shah*; it is famous for the so called *'Whispering Gallery'*.
- *Quli Qutub Shah* built the famous *Golcunda Fort*.

MUGHAL EMPIRE
(1526-1707 AD)

BABAR (1526-1530 AD)

- Babar was the founder of the Mughal Empire in India.
- On 21st April, 1526 the first Battle of Panipat took place between Babar and Ibrahim Lodhi, who was killed in the battle.
- Babar was the first one to use guns or artillery in a battle on the Indian soil.
- Babar defeated Rama Sanga of Mewar in the battle of Kanwah in A.D. 1527.
- Babar was a soldier-scholar and wrote his own autobiography called Babar Nama in Turkish language.

HUMAYUN (1530-1556 AD)

- Sher Shah defeated Humayun at *Chausa in A.D. 1539* and again at Kannauj in A.D. 1540.
- After losing his kingdom, Humayun became an exile for the next fifteen years.
- In 1555, Humayun defeated the Afghans and recovered the Mughal throne. After six months, he died in 1556 due to his fall from the staircase of his library.
- *Gulbadan Begum*, Humayun's half-sister wrote *Humayun-nama*.

SHER SHAH SURI

- The founder of the Sur dynasty was Sher Shah, whose original name was Farid.
- Sher Shah became the ruler of Delhi in 1540.

- Sher Shah organized a brilliant administrative system. The central government consisted of several departments.
- He built a new city on the banks of the river Yamuna near Delhi. Now the old fort called Purana Quila and its mosque is alone surviving.
- He built a Mausoleum at Sasaram, which is considered as one of the master pieces of Indian architecture.

AKBAR (1556-1605 AD)

Akbar

- When Akbar ascended the throne in A.D. 1556 he was only 14 years old. His guardian Bairam Khan served him as a faithful minister and tutor.
- Bairam Khan, along with Akbar met Hemu in the second Battle of Panipat in 1556. Hemu was initially successful, but lost his consciousness after an arrow hit him. Akbar killed him.
- In the Battle of Haldighati, Rana Pratap Singh was severely defeated by the Mughal army led by Man Singh in 1576.
- Akbar abolished the pilgrim tax and in 1562, he abolished Jaziya.
- Akbar evolved a new faith called Din-i-Illahi or Divine Faith.

JAHANGIR (1605-1627 AD)

- When Akbar died, Prince Salim succeeded with the title Jahangir (Conqueror of World) in 1605.
- Jahangir's eldest son, Khusrau, rebelled against him. He was arrested and put into prison. *Guru Arjun Dev, the fifth Sikh Guru* was executed by Jahangir.
- In 1611, Jahangir married Mehrunnisa who was known as Nurjahan (Light of World).

Jahangir

- Jahangir died in A.D. 1627.

General Knowledge

SHAHJAHAN (1628-1658 AD)

- The reign of Shahjahan is generally considered as the *Golden Age* of the Mughal period.
- Shahjahan is called as the *Prince of Builders*. He had built the Jama Masjid and *Red Fort* in Delhi and Taj Mahal in Agra.
- Fine arts like painting, music and literature reached high level of development during Shahjahan's time.

AURANGAZEB (1658-1707 AD)

- Aurangazeb was the last great Mughal ruler. He ascended the throne after killing his three brothers Dara, Shuja and Murad in a fratricidal war.
- Aurangazeb defeated Sikandar Shah of Bijapur and annexed his kingdom.
- Aurangazeb was against the Sikhs and he executed the ninth Sikh Guru Tegh Bahadur.
- He was called *Darvesh* or a *Zinda Pir*. He forbade *Sati*. Conquered Bijapur (AD 1686) and Golconda (AD 1687) and reimposed Jaziya and Pilgrim tax in AD 1679.
- He built *Biwi ka Makbara* on the tomb of his queen *Rabaud-Durani* at Aurangabad; *Moti Masjid* within Red Fort, Delhi; and the Jami or Badshahi Mosque at Lahore.
- Aurangazeb died in A.D. 1707.

LATER MUGHALS / FALL OF THE MUGHALS

Bahadur Shah (1707-1712)

- Assumed the title of *Shah Alam I*.

Jahandar Shah (1712-1713)

- First puppet Mughal emperor. He abolished *jaziya*.

Farrukhsiyar (1713-1719)

Mohammad Shah (1719-1748)

- Nadir Shah (*of Iran*) defeated him in the Battle of Karnal (1739) and took away *Peacock throne* and *Kohinoor diamond*.

Ahmad Shah (1748-1754)

Alamgir II (1754-1759), Shah Alam II (1759-1806)

Akbar II (1806-1837)

- He gave Ram Mohan Roy the title '*Raja*'. He sent Raja Ram Mohan Roy to London to seek a raise in his allowance.

Bahadur Shah II (1837-1857)

- He was confined by the British to the Red Fort. During the revolt of 1857, he was proclaimed the Emperor by the rebels. He was deported to Rangoon after that.

☞ **Literature of Mughal Period**

Author	Work
Babar	Tuzuk-i-Babari
Abul Fazal	Ain-i-Akbari, Akbarnamah
Jahangir	Tuzuk-i-Jahangir
Hamid	Padshahnama
Darashikoh	Majn-ul-Bahrain
Mirza Md Qasim	Alamgirnama

THE MARATHAS

SHIVAJI (1627-1680 AD)

- Shivaji was born at Shivner in 1627. His father was Shahji Bhonsle and mother Jija Bai.
- His religious teacher was Samarth Ramdas and guardian was Dadaji Kondadev.
- In 1674, Shivaji crowned himself at Raigarh and assumed the title Chatrapathi.
- *Ashtapradhan* (eight ministers) helped in administration. These were Peshwas, Sar-i-Naubat (Military), Mazumdar or

Amatya (Accounts); Waqenavis (Intelligence); Surnavis (Correspondence); *Dabir* or *Sumanta* (Ceremonies); *Nyayadhish* (Justice); and *Panditrao* (Charity).

- Successors of Shivaji were Shambhaji, Rajaram and *Shahu* (fought at Battle of Khed in AD 1708).

THE PESHWAS

- Balaji Vishwanath was the first Peshwa. He began his career as a small revenue official and became Peshwa in 1713.
- Baji Rao I was the eldest son of Balaji Vishwanath. He was considered as the "greatest exponent of guerilla tactics after Shivaji".
- It was during reign of Balaji Baji Rao (Nanasaheb) when the Marathas lost the Third Battle of Panipat.
- Baji Rao II (last Peshwa) was the first Maratha to have fled from the British attacks instead of fighting with them. Baji Rao II surrendered to Sir John Malcom.

THE SIKH

- Guru Nanak Dev was the founder of Sikhism, the religion that draws its elements from both Hinduism and Islam.

- Name of the ten Sikh Gurus and their works are given below:
    1. **Guru Nanak Dev (1469-1539AD):** The founder of Sikhism.
    2. **Guru Angad Dev (1504-1552AD):** Developed Gurmukhi.
    3. **Guru Amar Das (1479-1574AD):** Struggled against Sati system and Purdah system.
    4. **Guru Ram Das (1534-1581AD):** Founded Amritsar, the holy city of Sikhism.
    5. **Guru Arjun Dev (1563-1606AD):** He built the *Swarn Mandir* (Golden Temple).
    6. **Guru Hargobind (1595-1644 AD):** Established Akal Takht.
    7. **Guru Har Rai (1630-1661 AD)**
    8. **Guru Har Krishan (1656-1664 AD)**
    9. **Guru Tegh Bahadur (1621-1675 AD)**
    10. **Guru Gobind Singh (1666-1708 AD):** Founded the Khalsa and Sikh baptism, composed many poems, and nominated the Sikh sacred text as the final and enduring Guru.

MODERN INDIA

THE ADVENT OF THE EUROPEANS

THE PORTUGUESE

- Vasco-da-Gama, a Portuguese explorer, sailed through the route of cape of Good Hope and reached near Calicut on 20th May 1498 A.D. during the reign of King Zamorin (Hindu King of Calicut).
- Vasco-da-Gama founded a factory at Cannanore on his second visit to India in 1501. In due course, Calicut, Cochin and Cannanore became the Portuguese trading centres.
- Francisco Almeida came to India in 1505. He was the first Governor of Portuguese possessions in India.
- The real founder of Portuguese power in India was *Alfonso de Albuquerque*. He captured Goa from the rulers of Bijapur in 1510. It was made their headquarters.

THE DUTCH

- The United East India Company of the Netherlands founded a factory at

15

Masulipatnam in 1605. They built their first fort on the main land of India at Pulicut in 1609, near Madras (Chennai). They captured Nagapattinam from the Portuguese.

- They made Agra, Surat, Masulipatnam and Chinsura in Bengal as their trading centres.

THE DANES

- The Danish East India Company was established in 1616 in Denmark.
- They came to South India and founded a factory at Tranquebar (Tharangambadi) in 1620. They also made settlements at Serampore near Calcutta (Kolkata).

THE ENGLISH

- The English East India Company was formed in 1599 under a charter granted by Queen Elizabeth in 1600.
- The East India Company sent Sir William Hawkins to the court of the Mughal Emperor Jahangir in 1609 to obtain permission to erect a factory at Surat.
- In 1615, Sir Thomas Roe, another British merchant, came to Jahangir's court. He stayed for three years and succeeded in getting permission to set up their trading centres at Agra, Surat, Ahmedabad and Broach.
- In 1690, the British got permission from Aurangazeb to build a factory on the site of Calcutta. In 1696 a fort was built at that place. It was called Fort William.

THE FRENCH

- The French East India Company was established in 1664 under the inspiring and energetic leadership of Colbert, the economic adviser of the French King Louis XIV.
- In 1667, the first French factory was established at Surat by Francis Caron who was nominated as Director-General.
- French were defeated by English in *Battle of Wandiwash* (1760).

EAST INDIA COMPANY

- After the Battle of Plassey in 1757 and the Battle of Buxar in 1764, the East India Company became a political power.
- India was under the East India Company's rule till 1858 when it came under the direct administration of the British Crown.
- Robert Clive was the first Governor of Fort William under the Company's rule.

GOVERNOR-GENERALS OF BENGAL

Warren Hastings (1772-85 AD)

- In 1772, the Company appointed Warren Hastings as the Governor of Fort William.
- The Dual System introduced by Robert Clive was abolished by Warren Hastings.
- Warren Hastings was known for his expansionist policy. His administration witnessed the Rohilla War, the First Anglo-Maratha War and the Second Anglo-Mysore War.
- Pitt's India Act (1784) passed.

Lord Cornwallis (1786-93 AD)

- Cornwallis inaugurated the policy of making appointments mainly on the basis of merit thereby laying the foundation of the Indian Civil Service.
- Lord Cornwallis introduced Permanent Revenue Settlement.
- Tipu Sultan signed the Treaty of Srirangapatnam in 1792 with the British.

Sir John Shore (1793-98 AD)

- Played an important role in the introduction of Permanent Settlement.
- *Battle of Kharda* between the Nizams and the Marathas (1795).

Wellesley (1798-1805)

- Wellesley came to India with a determination to launch a forward policy that he adopted to achieve his object is known as the 'Subsidiary Alliance'.

- The Fourth Anglo-Mysore War started in 1799. The war was short and decisive. Tipu fought till his capital Srirangapatnam was captured and he himself was shot dead.
- Peshwa Baji Rao II signed the *Treaty of Bassein* with the British in 1802. It was a subsidiary treaty and the Peshwa was recognized as the head of the Maratha kingdom.
- The Treaty of Deogaon(1803) was signed between Bhonsle and Wellesley.

Lord Minto (1807-1813)

- Lord Minto concluded the Treaty of Amritsar with Ranjit Singh of Punjab in 1809.
- The Charter Act of 1813 was passed during this period.

Lord Hastings (1813-1823)

- Anglo Nepal War (1814-1816) and Treaty of Sagauli (1816).
- Third Maratha War (1817-18) dissolution of Maratha confederacy and creation of Bombay Presidency.
- He encouraged the freedom of the Press and abolished the censorship introduced in 1799.

GOVERNOR-GENERALS OF INDIA

Lord William Bentinck (1828-1835)

- Charter Act of 1833 was passed and he was made the first Governor-General of India. Before him, the designation was Governor-General of Bengal.
- The social reforms of William Bentinck made his name immortal in the history of British India. These include the abolition of *Sati*, the suppression of Thugs and the prevention of female infanticide.
- The Government Resolution in 1835 made English the official and literary language of India.

Lord Metcalfe (1835-36 AD)

- Known as liberator of press in India.

Lord Auckland (1836-42 AD)

- First Afghan War (1838-42), a disaster for the English.

Lord Ellenborough (1842-44 AD)

- Brought an end to Afghan war. War with Gwalior (1843) *Annexation of Sind* by Charles Napier (1843).

Lord Hardinge (1844-48 AD)

- First Anglo-Sikh War (1845-46) and Treaty of Lahore (1846). Give preference to English educated persons in employment.

Lord Dalhousie (1848-1856)

- The Doctrine of Lapse was applied by Dalhousie.
- The first railway line connecting Bombay with Thane was opened in 1853.

VICEROYS OF INDIA

Lord Canning (1856-62 AD)

- Lord Canning became the first Viceroy of India in 1858.
- Revolt of 1857, Mutiny took place. Indian Penal code 1860 was passed.

Lord Elgin (1862 AD)

- Wahabi Movement.

Lord John Lawrence (1864-69 AD)

- Established the *High Courts* at Calcutta, Bombay and Madras in 1865.
- Telegraphic communication was opened with Europe. Created the Indian Forest Department.

Lord Northbrooke (1872-76 AD)

- Kuka Rebellion in Punjab, Famine in Bihar.

Lord Lytton (1876-80)

- In 1878, the Vernacular Press Act was passed. This Act empowered a Magistrate to secure an undertaking from the editor, publisher and printer of a

General Knowledge

vernacular newspaper that nothing would be published against the English Government. This Act crushed the freedom of the Indian press.

- In 1878, the Arms Act was passed. This Act prevented the Indians to keep arms without appropriate license.
- Lord Lytton also held a Darbar at Delhi in 1877 in which Queen Victoria was declared as the Empress of India. This extravagant Darbar cost millions of ruppes.
- In 1878, the Statutory Civil Service was established exclusively for Indians.

Lord Rippon (1880-84 AD)

- Lord Ripon repealed the Vernacular Press Act and earned much popularity among Indians.
- Ripon appointed a Commission in 1882 under the chairmanship of Sir William Hunter.
- The Commission came to be known as the Hunter Commission. The Commission recommended for the expansion and improvement of the elementary education of the masses.
- Ripon was founder of local self-government in modern India.

Lord Dufferin (1884-88 AD)

- *Third Burmese War* (1885-86 AD). Establishment of the Indian National Congress in 1885.

Lord Lansdowne (1888-94 AD)

- Factory Act of 1891 granted weekly holiday and stipulated working hours for women and children.

Lord Elgin II (1894-99 AD)

- Southern uprisings of 1899. Great famine of 1896-1897 and Lyall Commission on famine was established.

Lord Curzon (1899-1905 AD)

- Curzon instituted in 1902, a Universities Commission to go into the entire question of university education in the country.
- On the basis of the findings and recommendations of the Commission, Curzon brought in the Indian Universities Act of 1904, which brought all the universities in India under the control of the government.

Lord Minto (1905-10 AD)

- Swadeshi Movement (1905-08); foundation of Muslim League (1906); Surat Session and split in the Congress (1907). Morley-Minto Reforms (1909).

Lord Hardinge (1910-16 AD)

- Capital shifted from Calcutta to Delhi (1911); Delhi Durbar; Partition of Bengal was cancelled. The Hindu Mahasabha was founded in 1915 by Pandit Madan Mohan Malaviya.

Lord Chelmsford (1916-21 AD)

- Gandhi returned to India (1915) and founded the Sabarmati Ashram (1916), Champaran Satyagraha, Satyagraha at Ahmedabad (1981), Kheda Satyagraha (1918).
- Rowlatt Act (March, 1919) and the Jallianwala Bagh Massacre (13th April, 1919).
- Khilafat Committee was formed and Khilafat Movement started (1919-20).
- Non-Cooperation Movement started (1920-22).

Lord Reading (1921-26)

- Moplah Rebellion (1921) took place. *Kakori Train* Robbery on 1st August, 1925. *Communal Riots* of 1923-25 in Multan, Amritsar, Delhi etc.

Lord Irwin (1926-31 AD)

- Lahore Session of Congress and *Poorna Swaraj* Declaration (1925).
- Simon Commission visited India in 1927. Congress passed the Indian Resolution in 1929.

- Dandi March (12th March, 1930). Civil Disobedience Movement (1930).
- First Round Table Conference was held in England in 1930. Gandhi-Irwin Pact.

Lord Willingdon (1931-36 AD)

- *Second Round Table Conference* in London in 1931 and *third* in 1932.

Lord Linlithgow (1936-43 AD)

- Congress Ministries resignation celebrated as *'Deliverance Day'* by the Muslim League (1939), the Lahore Resolution (23rd March, 1940) of the Muslim League demanding separate state for the Muslims. (It was at this session that Jinnah propounded his Two-Nation Theory). Outbreak of World War II in 1939. Cripps Mission in 1942. Quit India Movement (8th August, 1942).

Lord Wavell (1943-47 AD)

- Cabinet Mission Plan (16th May, 1946).
- First meeting of the Constituent Assembly was held on 9th December, 1946.
- Arranged the Shimla Conference on 25th June, 1945 with Indian National Congress and Muslim League failed.

Lord Mountbatten (March to Aug, 1947)

- Last viceroy of British India and the first Governor-General of free India.
- Partition of India decided by the 3rd June Plan or Mountbatten Plan.

NATIONAL MOVEMENT
(1885-1947)

INDIAN NATIONAL CONGRESS (1885)

- Allan Octavian Hume, a retired civil servant in the British Government took the initiative to form an all-India organization. Thus, the Indian National Congress was founded and its first session was held at Bombay in 1885. W.C. Banerjee was its first president. It was attended by 72 delegates from all over India.
- The second session was held in Calcutta in 1886 and the third in Madras in 1887.
- Between 1885 and 1905, the Congress leaders were moderates. The Moderates had faith in the British justice and goodwill. They were called moderates because they adopted peaceful and constitutional means to achieve their demands.
- In 1905, Gopal Krishna Gokhale founded the Servants of India Society to train Indians to dedicate their lives to the cause of the country.

Partition of Bengal (1905)

- By Lord Curzon on 16th October, 1905 through a royal proclamation, reducing the old province of Bengal in size by creating East Bengal and Assam out of the rest of Bengal.
- The partition of Bengal in 1905 provided a spark for the rise of extremism in the Indian National Movement.
- Curzon's real motives behind this partition were:
  - To break the growing strength of Bengali nationalism since Bengal was the base of Indian nationalism.
  - To divide the Hindus and Muslims in Bengal.
  - To show the enormous power of the British Government in doing whatever it liked.

Swadeshi Movement (1905)

- The Swadeshi Movement involved programmes like the boycott of government service, courts, schools and colleges and of foreign goods. It was both a political and economic movement.
- Lal, Bal, Pal and Aurobindo Ghosh played an important role.

General Knowledge 

Muslim League (1906)

- In December 1906, Muslim delegates from all over India met at Dacca for the Muslim Educational Conference.
- Taking advantage of this occasion, Nawab Salimullah of Dacca proposed the setting up of an organisation to look after the Muslim interests. The proposal was accepted.
- The All-India Muslim League was finally set up on December 30, 1906.

Minto Morley Reforms (1909)

- Minto, the Viceroy and Morley, the Secretary of State for India jointly proposed reforms to the Indian Councils. An Act, called the Indian Councils Act or the Minto-Morley Reforms Act was passed in 1909.
- A separate communal electorate was introduced for the Muslims.

The Lucknow Pact (1916)

- During the 1916 Congress session at Lucknow two major events occurred. The divided Congress became united. An understanding for joint action against the British was reached between the Congress and the Muslim League and it was called the Lucknow Pact.
- The signing of the Lucknow Pact by the Congress and the Muslim League in 1916 marked an important step in the Hindu-Muslim unity.

The Home Rule Movement (1916)

- Two Home Rule Leagues were established, one by B.G. Tilak at Poona in April 1916 and the other by Mrs. Annie Besant at Madras in September 1916.
- While Tilak's Movement concentrated on Maharashtra, Annie Besant's Movement covered the rest of the country.

August Declaration

- On 20 August, 1917, Montague, the Secretary of State in England, promised the gradual development of self-governing institutions in India.
- This August Declaration led to the end of the Home Rule Movement.

Rowlatt Act (1919)

- In 1917, a committee was set up under the presidentship of Sir Sydney Rowlatt to look into the militant Nationalist activities. On the basis of its report the Rowlatt Act was passed in March 1919 by the Central Legislative Council. As per this Act, any person could be arrested on the basis of suspicion. No appeal or petition could be filed against such arrests.
- This Act was called the Black Act and it was widely opposed. An all-India hartal was organized on 6 April, 1919.

Jallianwala Bagh Massacre (13 April, 1919)

- On 13th April, the Baisakhi day (harvest festival), a public meeting was organized at the Jallianwala Bagh (garden). Gen. Dyer marched in and without any warning opened fire on the crowd. The firing continued for about 10 to 15 minutes and it stopped only after the ammunition exhausted.
- According to official report 379 people were killed and 1137 wounded in the incident. There was a nationwide protest against this massacre and Rabindranath Tagore renounced his knighthood as a protest.

Khilafat Movement (1920)

- The chief cause of the Khilafat Movement was the defeat of Turkey in the First World War.
- The Muslims in India were upset over the British attitude against Turkey and launched the Khilafat Movement.
- Ali brothers, *Mohd Ali* and *Shaukat Ali* started this movement. It was jointly led by the Khilafat leaders and the Congress.

Non-Co-operation Movement (1920-22)

- Mahatma Gandhi announced his plan to begin Non-Cooperation with the government as a sequel to the Rowlatt Act, Jallianwala Bagh massacre and the Khilafat Movement. It was approved by the Indian National Congress at the Nagpur session in December, 1920.
- The Congress observed the Non-Co-operation movement in 1920. The main aim of this movement was to attain Swaraj through non-violent and peaceful means.
- The whole movement was abruptly called off on 11th February, 1922 by Gandhi following the Chauri-Chaura incident in the Gorakhpur district of U.P. Many top leaders of the country were stunned at this sudden suspension of the Non-Co-operation Movement.
- On 5th February an angry mob set fire to the police station at *Chauri-Chaura* and twenty two police men were burnt to death.

Swaraj Party

- Leaders like Motilal Nehru and Chittranjan Das formed a separate group within the Congress known as the Swaraj Party on 1 January, 1923.
- The Swarajists wanted to contest the council elections and wreck the government from within.

Simon Commission (1927)

- The Act of 1919 included a provision for its review after a lapse of ten years. However, the review commission under the chairmanship of Sir John Simon was appointed by the British Government two years earlier of its schedule in 1927.
- Indian leaders opposed the commission, as there were no Indians in it, they cried *Simon Go Back*.
- The government used brutal repression and at Lahore, *Lala Lajpat Rai* was severely beaten in lathi-charge.

Nehru Report (1928)

- The Secretary of State, Lord Birkenhead, challenged the Indians to produce a Constitution that would be acceptable to all. The challenge was accepted by the Congress, which convened an all party meeting on 28 February, 1928.
- A committee consisting of eight was constituted to draw up a blueprint for the future Constitution of India. It was headed by Motilal Nehru. The Report published by this Committee came to be known as the Nehru Report.

Lahore Session (1929)

- On Dec. 19, 1929, under the Presidentship of J.L. Nehru, the INC, as its Lahore session, declared Poorna Swaraj (Complete Independence) as its ultimate goal.
- On Dec. 31, 1929, the newly adopted tricolour flag was unfurled and Jan. 26, 1930 was fixed as the First Independence Day, which was to be celebrated every year.

Dandi March (1930)

- On 12th March, 1930, Gandhi began his famous March to Dandi with his chosen 79 followers to break the salt laws. He reached the coast of Dandi on 5 April, 1930 after marching a distance of 200 miles and on 6 April formally launched the Civil Disobedience Movement by breaking the salt laws.

Civil Disobedience Movement

- Countrywide mass participation by women.
- The Garhwal soldiers refused to fire on the people at Peshawar.

Round Table Conference

- The first Round Table Conference was held in November 1930 at London and it was boycotted by the Congress.
- On 8 March, 1931 the Gandhi-Irwin Pact was signed. As per this pact, Mahatma

General Knowledge 

Gandhi agreed to suspend the Civil-Disobedience Movement and participate in the Second-Round Table Conference.

- In September 1931, the Second Round Table Conference was held at London. Mahatma Gandhi participated in the Conference but returned to India disappointed.
- In January 1932, the Civil-Disobedience Movement was resumed.

Poona Pact (1932)

- The idea of separate electorate for the depressed classes was abandoned, but seats reserved for them in the provincial legislature were increased.
- Thus, Poona Pact agreed upon a joint electorate for upper and lower castes.

Demand for Pakistan

- *Chaudhary Rehmat Ali* gave the term *Pakistan* in 1933.
- In March 1940, the Muslim League demanded the creation of Pakistan.

Cripps Mission (1942)

- The British Government in its effort to secure Indian co-operation in the Second World War sent Sir Stafford Cripps to India on 23 March, 1942. This is known as Cripps Mission.
- The main recommendations of Cripps was the promise of Dominion Status to India.
- Congress rejected it. Gandhi called Cripp's proposals as a "Post-dated Cheque".

Quit India Movement (1942-1944)

- The All India Congress Committee met at Bombay on 8 August, 1942 and passed the famous Quit India Resolution. On the same day, Gandhi gave his call of 'do or die'.
- On 8th and 9th August, 1942, the government arrested all the prominent leaders of the Congress. Mahatma Gandhi was kept in prison at Poona.

Pandit Jawaharlal Nehru, Abul Kalam Azad, and other leaders were imprisoned in the Ahamednagar Fort.

- Quit India Movement was the final attempt for country's freedom.

Indian National Army (INA)

- On July 2, 1943, Subhash Chandra Bose reached Singapore and gave the rousing war cry of 'Dilli Chalo'. He was made the President of Indian Independence League and soon became the supreme commander of the Indian National Army. He gave the country the slogan of Jai Hind.
- INA had three fighting brigades names after Gandhi, Azad and Nehru. Rani of Jhansi Brigade was an exclusive women force. INA headquarters at Rangoon and Singapore.

Cabinet Mission (1946)

- The Cabinet Mission put forward a plan for solution of the constitutional problem. A proposal was envisaged for setting up an Interim Government, which would remain in office till a new government was elected on the basis of the new Constitution framed by the Constituent Assembly.
- Elections were held in July 1946 for the formation of a Constituent Assembly.
- Muslim league observed the *Direct Action Day* on 16 August, 1946.
- An Interim Government was formed under the leadership of Jawaharlal Nehru on 2 September, 1946.

Mountbatten Plan (1947)

- On 20 February 1947, Prime Minister Atlee announced in the House of Commons the definite intention of the British Government to transfer power to responsible Indian hands by a date not later than June 1948.
- Lord Mountbatten armed with vast powers became India's Viceroy on 24

March, 1947. The partition of India and the creation of Pakistan appeared inevitable to him.

- After extensive consultation Lord Mountbatten put forth the plan of partition of India on 3 June, 1947. The Congress and the Muslim League ultimately approved the Mountbatten Plan.

Indian Independence Act, 1947

- The salient features of this Act was the partition of the country into India and Pakistan would come into effect from 15 August, 1947.

- On 15th August, 1947 India, and on the 14th August Pakistan came into existence as two independent states.

- Lord Mountbatten was made the first Governor General of Independent India, whereas Mohammad Ali Jinnah became the first Governor General of Pakistan.

- C. Rajagopalachari became the first and last Indian Governor-General of India. When India became a Republic on 26 January, 1950 Dr. Rajendra Prasad became the first President of our country.

☞ Socio-Religious Movements and Organisation

Year	Place	Name of the Organisation	Founder
1815	Calcutta	Atmiya Sabha	Ram Mohan Roy
1828	Calcutta	Brahmo Samaj	Ram Mohan Roy
1829	Calcutta	Dharma Sabha	Radhakanta Dev
1839	Calcutta	Tattvabodhini Sabha	Debendranath Tagore
1840	Punjab	Nirankaris	Dayal Das, Darbara Singh, Rattan Chand etc.
1844	Surat	Manav Dharma Sabha	Durgaram Manchharam
1849	Bombay	Paramhansa Mandli	Dadoba Pandurung
1857	Punjab	Namdharis	Ram Singh
1861	Agra	Radha Swami Satsang	Tulsi Ram
1866	Calcutta	Brahmo Samaj of India	Keshab Chandra Sen
1866	Deoband	Dar-ul-Ulum	Maulana Hussain Ahmed
1867	Bombay	Prarthna Samaj	Atmaram Pandurung
1875	Bombay	Arya Samaj	Swami Dayanand Saraswati
1875	New York (USA)	Theosophical Society	Madam H.P. Blavatsky and Col. H.S. Olcott
1878	Calcutta	Sadharan Brahmo Samaj	Anand Mohan Bose
1884	Pune (Poona)	Deccan Education Society	G.G. Agarkar
1886	Aligarh	Muhammadan Educational Conference	Syed Ahmad Khan
1887	Bombay	Indian National Conference	M.G. Ranade
1887	Lahore	Deva Samaj	Shivnarayan Agnihotri
1894	Lucknow	Nadwah-ul-Ulama	Maulana Shibli Numani
1897	Belur	Ramakrishna Mission	Swami Vivekananda
1905	Bombay	Servents of Indian Society	Gopal Krishna Gokhale
1909	Pune (Poona)	Poona Seva Sadan	Mrs. Ramabai Ranade and G.K. Devadhar
1911	Bombay	Social Service League	N.M. Joshi
1914	Allahabad	Seva Samiti	H.N. Kunzru

General Knowledge

☞ Newspapers and Journals

● Bengal Gazette (1780) (India's first newspaper)	James Angustus Hikky
● Kesari	B.G. Tilak
● Maratha	B.G. Tilak
● Sudharak	G.K. Gokhale
● Amrit Bazar Patrika	Shishir Kumar Ghosh and Motilal Ghosh
● Yugantar	Bhupendranath Datta and Birender Kumar Ghosh
● Bombay Chronicle	Firoze Shah Mehta
● New India (Daily)	Annie Besant

☞ Books and Authors

● Causes of the Indian Mutiny	Sir Syed Ahmed Khan
● Ghulam Giri	Jyotiba Phule
● Anandmath	Bankim Chand Chatterjee
● Satyarth Prakash	Swami Dayanand
● Unhappy India	Lala Lajpat Rai
● India Divided	Dr. Rajendra Prasad
● The Discovery of India	J.L. Nehru
● Neel Darpan	Dinbandhu Mitra
● Hind Swaraj	M.K. Gandhi
● What Congress and Gandhi have done to the untouchables	Dr. B.R. Ambedkar

☞ Important Sayings

'Back to Vedas'	Dayanand Saraswati
'Dilli Chalo!'	Subhash Chandra Bose's battle cry of *Azad* Hind Fauj
'Do or Die'	Mahatma Gandhi (while launching Quit India movement in 1942)
'Give me blood and I will give you freedom'	Subhash Chandra Bose (in his address to soldiers of Azad Hind Fauj)
'My ultimate aim is to wipe every tear from every eye'	Jawaharlal Nehru
'Swaraj is my birthright and I will have it'	Bal Gangadhar Tilak
'Inqualab Zindabad'	Bhagat Singh
'Jai Jawan, Jai Kisan'	Lal Bahadur Shastri
'Sarfaroshi ki tamanna Ab Hamare Dil mein Hai'	Ram Prasad Bismill
'Saare Jahan Se Achcha, Hindustan Hamara'	Dr. Mohammed Iqbal
'Hindi, Hindu, Hindustan'	Bhartendu Harishchandra
'Vande Mataram'	Bankim Chandra Chatterjee

ART AND CULTURE

☞ Classical Dance

Dance	State	Famous Artists
Bharat Natyam	Tamil Nadu	Yamini Krishnamurthy, Rukmini Devi Arundale, Swapna Sundari, Sonal Mansingh, Vaijanti Mala, Mrinalini Sarabhai, Chandralekha, Indrani, Ram Gopal, Bal Saraswati
Kathakali	Kerala	Gopinath, K.K. Nayar, Kunju-Kurup, T.K. Chandu
Kuchipudi	Andhra Pradesh	Sapna Sundari, Raja Reddy, Shobha Nayar, Radha Reddy, Vedantam Satyanarayan, Vimpanti Chinna Satyam.
Kathak	North India	Birju Maharaj, Gopi Krishna, Shambhu Maharaj, Sitara Devi, Vishnu Sharma, Durga Lal, Shobhana Narayan
Odissi	Odisha	Kelucharan Mahapatra, Indrani Rehman, Madhavi Mudgal, Pratima Bedi, Samyukta Panigrahi, Sonal Mansingh, Debudas
Manipuri	Manipur	Uday Shankar, Bipin Singh, Suryamukhi, Darohra Jhaveri

☞ Famous Folk Dances

State	Folk Dance	State	Folk Dance
Andhra Pradesh	Dandari, Banjara	Kerala	Mohini Attam, Padayuni
Assam	Bihu, Keli Gopal, Sataria	Madhya Pradesh	Lota Nritya, Jawara
Bihar	Chhau, Magahi, Durga dance	Maharashtra	Tamasha, Dahi Handi, Gof, Deepak Dindi
W. Bengal	Kirtan, Kalatri, Asweabadh, Brita, Kalidance	Manipur	Dhol Cholam
Chhattisgarh	Saila, Karama, Bhagoria	Meghalaya	Nongakarem
Gujarat	Garba, Rasalila, Tippani, Dandia,	Nagaland	Bamboo dance
Haryana	Damyal, Lahoor	Odisha	Chhau, Maya Shabari, Dalachai
Himachal Pradesh	Dussehra dance, Hikat, Notio	Punjab	Gidda, Bhangra, Panihari
Jammu & Kashmir	Dumhal	Rajasthan	Thumar, Kathaputali, Tera Tali
Jharkhand	Jhau, Ghumakudia, Jadur, Sarhul, Soharai, Karama, Vaima, Loojhari, Jat-Jatin, Vidayat	Tamil Nadu	Terukalathu, Kabalatam, Kargam, Pulivesham
		Tripura	Hazagiri
		Uttar Pradesh	Rasalila, Nautanki, Thali, Dhurang, Jhumela, Huraka, Bol.
		Uttarakhand	Kajari, Karan
Karnataka	Yakshagan, Dolu Kunitha	Goa	Dhode Modini

MUSIC

Main Schools of Classical Music

- There are two main schools of classical music, namely, the Hindustani and the Carnatic. The Hindustani school of classical music is in vogue in north-western India, eastern India and northern parts of the South India.

Musical Instruments

- They are: Tabla, Mridangam, Pakhawaj, Chandai, Dholak, Veena, Sitar, Sarod, Gootuvadhyam, Sarangi, Flute, Nadaswaram, Shehnai, Shringi and Turahi.

General Knowledge

☞ **Musical Instruments and Artists**

Musical Instrument	Artists
Flute	Hari Prasad Chaurasia, Panna Lal Ghosh, T.R. Mahalingam, N. Ramani, Vijaya Raghava Rao
Tabla	Allah Rakha, Gudai Maharaj, Latif Khan, Zakir Hussain
Violin	Lalgudi Jayaraman, L. Subramaniam, M.S. Gopal Krishnan, S. Subrahmaniam, V.G. Jog, N. Rajan
Shehnai	Bismilla Khan, Imrat Khan
Sarod	Ali Akbar Khan, Amjad Ali Khan, Alauddin Khan, Saren Rani, Brij Narayan
Sitar	Pandit Ravishankar, Vilayat Khan
Santur	Shiv Kumar Sharma
Rudraveena	Zia Mohiuddin Dagar
Pakhawaj	Govind Rao, Anokhe Lal, Kanthi Maharaj
Mridanga	Palghat R. Raghu, U.S. Burman
Harmonium	Purushottam Walawakar, M. Dhaulpuri
Guitar	Pt. Vishnu Mohan Bhatt, Brij Bhushan Kalra
Ghatam	T.H. Vinayakaram
Janjira	V. Nagarajan
Symphony	Jubin Mehta

CULTURE CENTRES

- *National Gallery of Modern Art:* Set up in 1954, the National Gallery of Modern Arts, New Delhi, houses a valuable collection of works of art from distinguished Indian artist such as Raja Ravi Verma, Rabindranath Tagore, Nandlal Bose, Amrita Sher-Gil, Devi Prasad Roy Chowdhary, M.F. Husain, Biren Dey, J. Swaminathan etc.

- *National School of Drama:* The National school of Drama, New Delhi, set up in 1959, imparts training in dramatic arts.

- *National Archives of India:* Based at New Delhi, it is the largest and perhaps the best organised record repository in Asia.

- *Zonal Cultural Centres:* These centres have been set up with the objectives of arousing interest in the local cultures and making people aware of their cultural identity which transcends territorial bounds and forms India's rich composite culture. The seven zonal cultural centres are : (1) North Zone Cultural Central, Patiala; (2) East Zone Cultural Centre, Shanti Niketan; (3) South Zone Cultural Centre, Thanjavur; (4) West Zone Cultural Centre, Udaipur; (5) North-Central Zone Cultural Centre, Allahabad; (6) North-East Zone Cultural Centre, Dimapur; and (7) South-Central Zone cultural Centre, Nagpur.

SCULPTURE

- Archaeological Survey of India, set up in 1861, is responsible for preservation and maintenance of sculptures and historical monuments and manages a number of archaeological museums.

- National Archives of India, established in 1891, it is the official custodian of all non-current records of permanent value of the Government of India and its predecessor bodies.

 General Knowledge

GEOGRAPHY

WORLD GEOGRAPHY

THE UNIVERSE

- Existing matter and energy are together known as **Universe.**

GALAXY

- A galaxy is a huge system of billions of stars and clouds of dust and gases.
- Our solar system is a part of *MilkyWay* galaxy.
- There are millions of galaxies that make the Universe.

STARS

- Stars account for 98 per cent of the matter in a galaxy. The stars nearest to the earth are *Proxima Centauri, Alpha Centauri, Barnard's Star, Sirius* and so on. Of these, *Sirius* is the brightest.

LIGHT YEAR

- Light year is the distance travelled by light in one year at a speed of 2,99,792.5 km. per second.

SOLAR SYSTEM

- The Sun, eight planets, satellites and some other celestial bodies known as asteroids and meteoroids form the solar system.

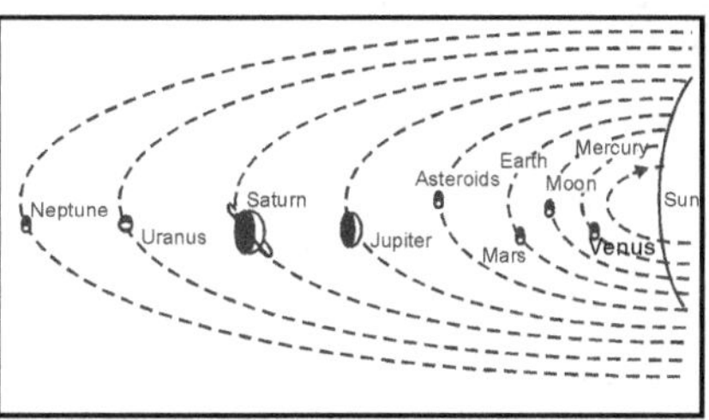

SUN

- The Sun is in the centre of the solar system.
- The Sun is a mixture of gases. It consists of 92% hydrogen, 7.8% helium and 0.2% other gases.
- The Sun is about 150 million km away from the earth.
- The sun is an ultimate source of energy for life on Earth.
- Sunlight takes 8 min 16.6 sec to reach earth.

☞ Facts about Sun

Diameter—1.392×10^6 km
Volume—1.304×10^6 times the volume of earth
Temperature—6000°C at surface and 15 million degree C at the centre
Relative density—1.4
Gravitational Pull—28 times the gravitational pull of the earth

☞ **Facts about Planets**

Closest to Sun	Mercury
Farthest from Sun	Neptune
Heaviest	Jupiter
Hottest	Venus
Inner	Mercury, Venus, Earth, Mars
Largest	Jupiter
Smallest	Mercury
Moons, None	Mercury, Venus
Moon; Largest	Ganymede (Jupiter), larger than Mercury
Nearest to Earth	Venus
Orbits; Order	Mercury (closest to Sun), Venus, Earth, Mars, Jupiter, Saturn, Uranus, Neptune.
Rings/largest number	Saturn
Spin; Backwards	Venus (East to West)

COMETS

- It has a head and a tail. Its tail originates only when it gets closer to the sun. The tail can be 20-30 million km long. It always point away from the sun because of the force exerted by solar wind and radiation on the cometory material.

THE EARTH

- The earth is the third nearest planet to the Sun.

- From the outer space, the earth appears blue because its two-thirds surface is covered by water. It is, therefore, called a blue planet.

- It is the densest of all planets.

- Rotation is the movement of the earth on its axis. Due to this rotation, day and night occur.

- The earth takes about 23 hours 56 minutes and 4 seconds to complete one rotation around its axis.

- Earth takes 365¼ days (one year) to revolve around the sun.

THE EARTH: FACTS AND FIGURES

- *Mass of Earth*—5.880×10^{21} tons
- *Density of Earth*—5.517 times that of water • *Volume of Earth*—1.083×10^{11} cubic km • *Equatorial circumference*—4.007×104 km • *Polar Diameter*—12,714 km • *Equatorial Diameter*—12756 km • *Polar or Meridional circumference*—4.0×10^4 km • *Estimated Age*—At least 4600 million years • *Land Surface*—148,951,000 sq km • *Water Surface*—361,150,000 sq km (71 per cent of total area) • *Highest Point of the land surface*—Mt. Everest (8,848 metres) • *Lowest point of the land surface*—Shores of the Dead Sea (396 metres below the sea level) • *Greatest Ocean depth*—Mariana Trench, East of Philippines (11,033 metres below the sea level)

THE MOON

- Earth has only one satellite, that is, the moon.

- Its diameter is only one-quarter that of the earth. It is about 3,84,400 km away from us.

- The moon moves around the earth in about 27 days. It takes exactly the same time to complete one spin. As a result, only one side of the moon (only 59% of its surface) is visible to us on the earth.

- Moonlight takes 1.3 sec. to reach earth.

LATITUDE

- Imaginary lines drawn parallel to the equator. Measured as an angle whose apex is at the centre of the earth.

- The equator represents 0° latitude, while the North Pole is 90°N and the South Pole 90°S.

- 23½°N represents Tropic of Cancer while 23½°S represents Tropic of Capricorn.

LONGITUDE

- It is the angular distance measured from the centre of the earth. On the globe the lines of longitude are drawn as a series of semicircles that extend from the North Pole to the South Pole through the equator. They are also called meridians.

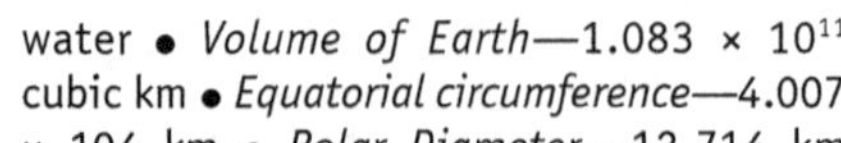 **General Knowledge**

- The distance between any two meridians is not equal. At the equator, 1 degree = 111 km. At 30°N or S, it is 96.5 km. It goes on decreasing this way until it is zero at the poles.

INTERNATIONAL DATE LINE

- It is the 180° meridian running over the Pacific Ocean, deviating at Aleutian Islands, Fiji, Samoa and Gilbert Islands.
- Travellers crossing the Date Line from west to east repeat a day and travellers crossing it from east to west lose a day.

INDIAN STANDARD TIME (IST)

- Indian Standard Time is calculated on the basis of 82.5°E longitude which passes through Uttar Pradesh, Madhya Pradesh, Odisha, Chattisgarh and Andhra Pradesh.

ECLIPSES

- Sun is the only source of light for both the Earth and Moon. Eclipses occur when the light thus received is either blocked by the earth or by the Moon.
- Eclipses occur when either the Earth moves behind the Moon's shadow or the Moon moves behind the Earth's shadow.

LUNAR ECLIPSE

- Lunar eclipses occur only when the following conditions are met.
  1. The Sun, Earth and Moon must be aligned in a straight line.
  2. The Earth must be positioned between the Sun and the Moon.
  3. The Moon must be in its full phase (Full Moon).

SOLAR ECLIPSE

- Solar eclipses occur only when the following conditions are met.
  1. The Sun, Earth and Moon must be aligned in a straight line.
  2. The Moon must be positioned between the Sun and the Earth.
  3. Must be a New Moon day.

ROCKS

- Rocks are composed of many minerals such as silica, aluminum, iron and magnesium. The nature of the rock is determined by the presence of its minerals.
- Rocks can be classified into three types **1.** *Igneous rocks* are formed by magma that reaches the earth's surface along deep cracks and at volcanic vents. e.g., Mica, Granite etc. **2.** *Sedimentary rocks* are formed by the accumulation and cementation of mud, silt, or sand derived from weathered igneous rock fragments. e.g., Gravel, Peat, Gypsum etc. **3.** *Metamorphic rocks* are igneous or sedimentary rocks that have been altered by heat and/or pressure, either because they have been buried and folded deep in the crust, or because they have come into contact with molten igneous rock, e.g., Gneiss, Marble, Quartzite etc.

VOLCANOES

Sudden eruption of hot magma (molten rock), gases, ash and other material from inside the Earth to its surface.

- *Active* which erupts frequently, e.g., Mauna Loa (Hawaii), Etna (Sicily), Vesuvius (Italy), Stromboli (Mediterranean Sea).
- *Dormand* Not erupted for quite sometime, e.g., Fujiyama (Japan), Krakatoa (Indonesia), Barren Island (Andamans).
- *Extinct* Not erupted for several centuries, e.g., Arthur's Seat, Edinburgh, Scotland.

EARTHQUAKES

- Earthquakes are a form of wave energy that is transferred through bedrock. It is transmitted from the point of the earthquake focus, as spherical seismic waves. They travel in all directions outward.
- The intensity of earthquake waves is recorded by *Seismograph*.

General Knowledge

LANDFORMS

- There are three major landforms: mountains, plateaus and plains.

MOUNTAINS

- A mountain can be defined as an area of land that rises abruptly from the surrounding region.
- There are three types of mountains- *Fold Mountains, Block Mountains* and the **Volcanic Mountains**.
- Himalayas, Alps, Andes, Rockies, Atlas, etc are examples of Fold Mountains.
- The Aravali range in India is one of the oldest **fold mountain** systems in the world.
- The Rhine valley and the Vosges mountain in Europe are examples of such mountain systems.
- Volcanic mountains are formed due to volcanic activity.
- Mt. Kilimanjaro in Africa and Mt. Fujiyama in Japan are examples of such mountains.

☞ **Major Mountain Ranges of the World**

Range	Location	Highest Peak (m)	Length (km)
Andes	South America	6,960	7,200
Himalayas-Karakoram-Hindukush	South Central Asia	8,848	4,800
Rockies	North America	4,401	4,800
Great Dividing Range	East Australia	2,228	3,600
Western Ghat	Western India	2,637	1,610
Caucasus	Europe	5,642	1,200
Alaska	USA	6,194	1,130
Alps	Europe	4,808	1,050
Apennines	Europe	2,912	—
Ural	Asia	1,895	—
Atlas	North West Africa	—	1,930

PLATEAUS

- A plateau is an elevated flat land. It is a flat-topped table land standing above the surrounding area.

☞ **Principal Mountain Peaks of the World**

	Mountains	Height in Metres
1.	Mount Everest	8,848
2.	K-2 (Godwin Austen)	8,611
3.	Kanchenjunga	8,598
4.	Lhotse	8,511
5.	Makalu I	8,481
6.	Dhaulagiri I	8,167
7.	Mansalu I	8,156
8.	Chollyo	8,153
9.	Nanga Parbat	8,124
10.	Annapurna I	8,091
11.	Gasherbrum I	8,068
12.	Broad Peak I	8,047
13.	Gasherbrum II	8,034
14.	Shisha Pangma (Gosainthan)	8,014
15.	Gasherbrum III	7,952

PLAINS

- A relatively low-lying and flat land surface with least difference between its highest and lowest points is called a Plain.

ATMOSPHERE

- Atmosphere is a mixture of different gases and it envelopes the earth all round. It contains life-giving gases like oxygen for humans and animals and carbon dioxide for plants.

☞ **Permanent Gases of the Atmosphere**

Constituent	Formula	Percentage by Volume
Nitrogen	N_2	78.08
Oxygen	O_2	20.95
Argon	Ar	0.93
Carbon dioxide	CO_2	0.036
Neon	Ne	0.002
Helium	He	0.0005
Krypton	Kr	0.001
Xenon	Xe	0.00009
Hydrogen	H_2	0.00005

 General Knowledge

- Due to horizontal differences in air pressure, air flows from areas of high pressure to areas of low pressure. **Horizontal movement** of the air is called wind.

Classification of winds

Winds may be classified into 4 types:

1. Permanent or Planetary winds
2. Periodic or Seasonal winds
3. Variable winds
4. Local winds

DESERT VEGETATION

- Deserts may be classified into two types: (a) Hot deserts and (b) Cold deserts.

  Hot deserts—Such vegetation are found in the Sahara and Kalahari deserts of Africa, Thar desert of India and the great Australian desert.

  Cold deserts—Cold deserts are found in the higher latitudes where there is absence of rainfall.

OCEANS

- Oceans of the world is classified into four groups: the Pacific, the Atlantic, the Arctic and the Indian.

- The Pacific is the largest ocean, being twice the size of the Atlantic. It covers about a third of the Earth's surface, and contains more than half the water on the planet.

☞ **Oceans of the World**

Names	Area (Sq. Km.)	Greatest Depth
Pacific	166,240000	Mariana Trench
Atlantic	86,560000	Puerto Rico Trench
Indian	73430000	Java Trench
Arctic	13230000	—

☞ **Major Rivers of the World**

River	Origin	Falls in	Length (Km.)
Nile	Victoria lake	Mediterranean Sea	6,650
Amazon	Andes (Peru)	Atlantic Ocean	6,428
Yangtze	Tibetan Kiang Plateau	China Sea	6,300
Mississippi Missouri	Itaska lake (USA)	Gulf of Mexico (USA)	6,275
Yenisei	Tannu-Ola Mts.	Arctic Ocean	5,539
Hoang Ho	Kunlun Mts.	Gulf of Chibli	5,464
Ob	Altai Mts., Russia	Gulf of Ob	5,410
Congo	Lualaba & Luapula rivers	Atlantic Ocean	4,700
Amur	Northeast China	Sea of Okhotsk	4,444
Lena	Baikal Mts	Laptev Sea	4,400
Mekong	Tibetan Highlands	South China Sea	4,350
Mackenzie	Great Slave Lake	Beaufort Sea	4,241
Niger	Guinea	Gulf of Guinea	4,200

☞ **Major Gulfs of the World**

Names	Area (Sq. Km.)	Names	Areas (Sq. Km.)
Gulf of Mexico	15,44,000	Gulf of St. Lawrence	2,37,000
Gulf of Hudson	12,33,000	Gulf of California	1,62,000
Arabian Gulf	2,38,000	English Channel	89,900

☞ Important Straits of the World

Straits	Water Bodies joined	Area
Bab-al-Mandeb	Red Sea & Arabian Sea	Arabia & Africa
Bering	Arctic Ocean & Bering Sea	Alaska & Asia
Bosphorus	Black Sea & Marmara Sea	Turkey
Dover	North Sea & Atlantic Ocean	England & Europe
Florida	Gulf of Mexico & Atlantic Ocean	Florida & Bahamas Islands
Gibralter	Mediterranean Sea & Atlantic Ocean	Spain & Africa
Malacca	Java Sea & Bay of Bengal	India & Indonesia
Palk	Bay of Bengal & Indian Ocean	India & Sri Lanka
Magellan	South Pacific & South Atlantic Ocean	Chile
Sunda	Java Sea & Indian Ocean	Indonesia

☞ Important Lakes of the World

Lake	Location	Area (Sq. Km.)
Caspian	Russia and CIS	371000
Superior	Canada and USA	82414
Victoria	Tanzania (Africa)	69485
Huron	Canada and USA	59596
Michigan	USA	58016
Tanganyika	Africa	32892
Baikal	Russia (CIS)	31502
Great Bear	Canada	31080
Malawi	Malawi (Tanzania)	30044
Great Slave	Canada	28438

☞ Highest Waterfalls of the World

Name(s) (Foreign)	Location
Angel (Salto Angel)	Canaima Nat'l Park, Venezuela
Tugela	Natal Nat'l Park, South Africa
Utigord (Utigordsfoss)	Norway
Monge (Mongefoss)	Marstein, Norway
Gocta Cataracts	Chachapoyas, Peru
Mutarazi (Mtarazi)	Nyanga Nat'l Park, Zimbabwe
Yosemite	Yosemite Nat'l Park, California, U.S.
Espelands (Espelandsfoss)	Hardanger Fjord, Norway
Lower Mar Valley (Ostra Mardolafoss)	Eikesdal, Norway
Tyssestrengene	Odda, Norway

☞ Important Cities on River Banks (World)

City	Country	River
Adelaide	Australia	Torrens
Amsterdam	Netherlands	Amsel
Alexandria	Egypt	Nile
Ankara	Turkey	Kazil
Bangkok	Thailand	Chao Praya
Basra	Iraq	Eupharates and Tigris
Baghdad	Iraq	Tigris
Berlin	Germany	Spree
Bonn	Germany	Rhine
Budapest	Hungary	Danube
Bristol	UK	Avon
Buenos Aires	Argentina	Laplata
Chittagong	Bangladesh	Majyani
Canton	China	Si-Kiang
Cairo	Egypt	Nile
Chung King	China	Yang-tse-kiang
Cologne	Germany	Rhine
Dandzing	Germany	Vistula
Dresden	Germany	Elbe
Dublin	Ireland	Liffy
Hamburg	Germany	Elbe
Kabul	Afghanistan	Kabul
Karachi	Pakistan	Indus
Khortoum	Sudan	Confluence of Blue & White Nile
Lahore	Pakistan	Ravi
Leningrad	Russia	Neva
Lisbon	Portugal	Tagus
Liverpool	England	Messey
London	England	Thames

City	Country	River
Moscow	Russia	Moskva
Montreal	Canada	St. Lawrence
Nanking	China	Yang-tse-kiang
New Orleans	U.S.A.	Mississipi
New York	U.S.A.	Hudson
Ottawa	Canada	Ottawa
Paris	France	Seine
Philadelphia	U.S.A	Delaware
Perth	Australia	Swan
Prague	Czech Republic	Vitava
Quebec	Canada	SI. Lawrence
Rome	Italy	Tiber
Rotterdam	The Netherlands	New Moss
Stalingrad	Russia	Volga
Shanghai	China	Yang-tse-kiang
Sidney	Australia	Darling
Saint Louis	U.S.A	Mississippi
Tokyo	Japan	Arakava
Vienna	Austria	Danube
Warsaw	Poland	Vistula
Washington D.C.	U.S.A.	Potomac
Yangoon	Myanmar	Irawaddy

☞ World's Geographical Surnames

City of Sky-scrapers—New York
City of Seven Hills—Rome
City of Dreaming Spires—Oxford
City of Golden Gate—San Francisco
City of Magnificent Buildings—Washington D.C.
City of Eternal Springs—Quito (S. America)
China's Sorrow—Hwang Ho
Cockpit of Europe—Belgium
Dark Continent—Africa
Emerald Isle—Ireland
Eternal City—Rome
Empire City—New York
Forbidden City—Lhasa (Tibet)
Garden City—Chicago
Gate of Tears—Strait of Bab-el-Mandeb
Gift of the Nile—Egypt
Granite City—Aberdeen (Scotland)
Hermit Kingdom—Korea
Herring Pond—Atlantic Ocean
Holy Land—Jerusalem

Island Continent—Australia
Islands of Cloves—Zanzibar
Isle of Pearls—Bahrein (Persian Gulf)
Key to the Mediterranean—Gibralter
Land of Cakes—Scotland
Land of Golden Fleece—Australia
Land of Maple Leaf—Canada
Land of Morning Calm—Korea
Land of Midnight Sun—Norway
Land of the Thousand Lakes—Finland
Land of the Thunderbolt—Bhutan
Land of White Elephant—Thailand
Land of Thousand Elephants—Laos
Land of Rising Sun—Japan
Loneliest Island—Tristan De Gunha (Mid-Atlantic)
Manchester of Japan—Osaka
Pillars of Hercules—Strait of Gibraltar
Pearl of the Antilles—Cuba
Playground of Europe—Switzerland
Quaker City—Philadelphia
Queen of the Adriatic—Venice
Roof of the World—The Pamirs, Central Asia
Sugar bowl of the world—Cuba
Venice of the North—Stockholm
Windy City—Chicago
Whiteman's grave—Guinea Coast of Africa
Yellow River—Huang Ho (China)
Sickman of Europe—Turkey

☞ Agriculture: Major Producers

Rice—China, India, Indonesia, Bangladesh, Vietnam
Wheat—China, India, USA, Russia, France
Maize—USA, China, Brazil, Mexico, Argentina
Groundnut—China, India, Nigeria, USA, Indonesia
Tea—India, China, Sri Lanka, Kenya, Turkey
Cotton—China, USA, India, Pakistan, Brazil
Rubber—Indonesia, Thailand, Malaysia, India, China
Coffee—Brazil, Vietnam, Indonesia, Colombia, Mexico
Pulses Total—Brazil, India, China, Myanmar, Mexico

General Knowledge 

Durand Line	Pakistan & Afghanistan	**Hindenberg Line**	Poland & Germany (at the time of First World War)
MacMohan Line	India & China		
Radcliff Line	India & Pakistan	**38th Parallel**	North & South Korea
Maginot Line	France & Germany	**49th Parallel**	USA & Canada
Oder Niesse Line	Germany & Poland		

☞ **Continents: Some Facts**

Continent	Biggest Counrty	Highest Peak	Longest River
Asia	China	Mt. Everest (8848 m)	Yangtze Kiang
Africa	Algeria	Mt. Kilimanjaro (5895 m)	Nile
North America	Canada	Mt. Mckinley (6194 m)	Mississippi Missouri
South America	Brazil	Mt. Acancagua (6960 m)	Amazon
Europe	Russia	Mt. Elbrus (5642 m)	Ob
Australia	Australia	Mt. Coscuisco (2228 m)	Darling
Antarctica	—	Vinson Massif (5140 m)	—

INDIAN GEOGRAPHY

AREA AND LOCATION

- India is in the southern parts of the Asian continent. In the west of India lies the Arabian Peninsula while in the east lies the Indo-China Peninsula.
- India extends between 8°4' N and 37°6' N latitudes and between 68°7' E and 97°2' E longitudes.
- India, has a total geographic area of 32,87,263 sq. km. This is only 2.42 % of the total geographic area of the world but holds 16 per cent of the world's population.
- The 23½°N, which is the Tropic of Cancer, runs across the country.
- India has a length of 3214 km from north to south and 2933 km from east to west. It has a land frontier of 15200 km.
- The total length of the coastline of the mainland, Lakshadweep Islands and Andaman and Nicobar Islands is 7,516.6 km.
- India ranks seventh among the countries of the world, in terms of the geographical extent.

- India is bordered on three sides by water and on one by land, it is also a peninsula.
- India shares its common border with Afghanistan and Pakistan in the north-west, China and Bhutan in the north, and Bangladesh in the east. In the south, Sri Lanka is separated from India by a strait, known as the Palk Strait.
- There are 29 States, and 6 Union Territories and 1 National Capital Territory (Delhi) in India.
- 82°30' E longitude is considered as the Indian Standard Meridian. The local time of this longitude is taken as the Indian Standard Time (IST). This is 5½ hours ahead of the Greenwich Mean Time.

THE INDIAN STATES ON INTERNATIONAL BOUNDARIES ARE:

- ***Bordering Pakistan:*** Jammu and Kashmir, Punjab, Rajasthan, Gujarat.
- ***Bordering China:*** Jammu and Kashmir, Himachal Pradesh, Uttarakhand, Sikkim, Arunachal Pradesh.
- ***Bordering Nepal:*** Bihar, Uttarakhand, UP, Sikkim, West Bengal.

- *Bordering Bangladesh:* West Bengal, Mizoram, Meghalaya, Tripura, Assam (Asom).
- *Bordering Bhutan:* West Bengal, Sikkim, Arunachal Pradesh, Assam (Asom).
- *Bordering Myanmar:* Arunachal Pradesh, Nagaland, Manipur, Mizoram.
- *Bordering Afghanistan:* Jammu and Kashmir (Pakistan-occupied area).

☞ Important Passes

Kashmir	Burzi-La, Joji-La
Himachal Pradesh	Bara La, Cha-La, Shipki-La
Uttarakhand	Niti-La, Lipu-Lekh-La
Sikkim	Jelep-La, Nathu-La
Arunachal Pradesh	Bomdi-La

☞ Heighest Mountain Peaks of India

Peaks	Elevation* (in mts.)
Godwin Austin (K2)	8611*
Kanchenjunga	8598
Nanga Parvat	8126*
Gasherbrum	8068*
Broad Peak	8047*
Dastegil	7885*
Masherbrum (East)	7821*
Nanda Devi	7817
Masherbrum (West)	7806*
Rakoposhi	7788*
Kamet	7756
Saser Kangdi	7672

- *Above mean sea level in metres.*
- ** Situated in Pak occupied Kashmir (PoK).*

☞ Towns at River Banks

Town	River
Agra	Yamuna
Allahabad	Confluence of the Ganges and the Yamuna
Ayodhya	Saryu
Badrinath	Alaknanda
Kolkata	Hooghly
Cuttuck	Mahanadi
Delhi	Yamuna
Dibrugarh	Brahmaputra
Ferozepur	Satluj

Town	River
Guwahati	Brahmaputra
Hardwar	The Ganges
Hyderabad	Musi
Jabalpur	Narmada
Kanpur	The Ganges
Kota	Chambal
Kurnool	Tungbhadra
Lucknow	Gomti
Ludhiana	Sutlej
Nasik	Godavari
Pandharpur	Bhima
Patna	The Ganges
Sambalpur	Mahanadi
Srinagar	Jhelum
Srirangapattam	Cauveri
Surat	Tapti
Varanasi	The Ganges
Vijaywada	Krishna

☞ Waterfalls of India

Waterfall	Hgt (Mt.)	River	State
Jog/Gersoppa	260	Sharavati	Karnataka
Rakim Kund	168	Gaighat	Bihar
Chachai	127	Bihad	Madhya Pradesh
Kevti	98	Mahanadi	Madhya Pradesh
Sivasamudram	90	Cauveri	Karnataka
Kunchikal	455	Varani	Karnataka

☞ Important Lakes of India

Name of lake	State
Pulicat Lake	Tamil Nadu & Andhra Pradesh Border
Sambhar Lake	Rajasthan
Tso Moriri Lake	Jammu & Kashmir
Vembanad Lake	Kerala
Wular & Dal Lakes	Jammu and Kashmir
Chilka Lake	Odisha
Kolleru Lake	Andhra Pradesh
Loktak Lake	Manipur
Lonar Lake	Maharashtra
Pangong Lake	Jammu and Kashmir

General Knowledge

☞ **Rivers of India**

Name	Originates From	Falls Into
Yamuna	Yamunotri	Ganga
Chambal	Singar Chouri Peak, Vindhyan escarpment	Yamuna
Ghaghara	Matsatung Glacier	Ganga
Kosi	Near Gosain Dham Peak	Ganga
Sabarmati	Aravalis	Gulf of Khambat
Krishna	Western Ghats	Bay of Bengal
Godavari	Nasik district in Maharashtra	Bay of Bengal
Caurey	Brahmagir Range of Western Ghats	Bay of Bengal
Tungabharda	Western Ghats	Krishna
Ganges	Combines Sources	Bay of Bengal
Sutlej	Mansarovar Rakas lakes	Chenab
Indus	Near Mansarovar Lake	Arabian Sea
Ravi	Kullu Hills near Rohtang Pass	Chenab
Beas	Near Rohtang Pass	Sutlej
Jhelum	Verinag in Kashmir	Chenab
Son	Amarkantak	Ganga
Brahmaputra	Near Mansarovar Lake	Bay of Bengal
Narmada	Amarkantak	Gulf of Khambat
Tapti	Betul District in Madhya Pradesh	Gulf of Khambat
Mahanadi	Raipur District in Chhattisgarh	Bay of Bengal
Luni	Aravallis	Rann of Kuchchh
Ghaggar	Himalayas	Near Fatehabad
Betwa	Vindhyanchal	Yamuna

☞ **Geographical Surnames**

Bengal's Sorrow	Damodar River	City of Lakes	Srinagar
City of Palaces	Kolkata	Twin City	Hyderabad-Secunderabad
Gateway of India	Mumbai		
Pink City	Jaipur	City of Seven Islands	Mumbai
Paris of India	Jaipur	Diamond Harbour	Kolkata
Manchester of India	Ahmedabad	Switzerland of India	Kashmir
Kashmir of South	Kerala	Rice Bowl	Chhattisgarh
Son of Sea	Lakshadweep	Fruit Bowl	Himachal Pradesh
Queen of Mountains	Mussourie	Ganga of South	Cauvery
Iron City	Jamshedpur	Pitsburg of India	Jamshedpur
Hollywood of India	Mumbai	City of Bridges	Srinagar
Scotland of East	Meghalaya	Residence of God	Allahabad
City of Nababs	Lucknow	A Cross-road (Quadrivial) of National Highways	Kanpur
City of Temples & Ghats	Varanasi	Heart of India	Delhi
Land of Five Rivers	Punjab	Black River	Sharda
City of Golden Temple	Amritsar	City of Festivals	Madurai
Garden of India	Bangaluru	Queen of Deccan	Pune
Spice Garden of India	Kerala	Sorrow of Bihar	Kosi River

 **General Knowledge**

S.No.	Name of Project	Related State	River
1.	Bargi Project	Madhya Pradesh	Bargi
2.	Beas	Joint Venture of Haryana, Punjab and Rajasthan	Beas
3.	Bhadra	Karnakata	Bhadra
4.	Bhakra Nangal	Haryana, Punjab and Rajasthan	Sutluj
5.	Bhima I	Maharashtra	Pawana
6.	Bhima II	Maharashtra	Krishna
7.	Chambal	Joint Project of M.P. and Rajasthan	Chambal
8.	Damodar Valley Project	West Bengal and Bihar	Damodar
9.	Dulhasti Power Project	Jammu and Kashmir	Chenab
10.	Farakka	West Bengal	Hooghly
11.	Gandak	Bihar and U.P.	Gandak
12.	Ghataprabha	Karnataka	Ghataprabha
13.	Hasdeo Bango Project	Madhya Pradesh, Chhattisgarh	Hasdeo
14.	Hirakud	Odisha	Mahanadi
15.	Jayakwadi	Maharashtra	Godavari
16.	Kakrapara	Gujarat	Tapti
17.	Kangsbati	West Bengal	Kangsbati and Kumari
18.	Karjan	Gujarat	Karjan
19.	Kosi	Bihar	Kosi
20.	Koyana	Maharashtra	Koyana
21.	Krishna Project	Maharashtra	Krishna
22.	Kukadi	Maharashtra	Kukadi
23.	Left Bank Ghagra Canal	Uttar Pradesh	Ghagra
24.	Madhya Ganga Canal	Uttar Pradesh	Ganga
25.	Mahanadi Delta Scheme	Odisha	(The irrigation scheme will utilise releases from Hirakund Reservoir)
26.	Mahi	Gujarat	Mahi
27.	Malaprabha	Karnataka	Malaprabha
28.	Mayurakshi	West Bengal	Mayurakshi
29.	Nagarjunasagar	Andhra Pradesh	Krishna
30.	Panam	Gujarat	Panam
31.	Parambikulam Aliyar	Tamil Nadu and Kerala	Perimbikulam
32.	Pochampad	Andhra Pradesh	Godavari
33.	Pong Dam	Punjab	Beas
34.	Ramganga	Uttarakhand	Ramganga
35.	Ranjit Sagar Dam (Thein Dam)	Punjab	Ravi
36.	Rihand	Uttar Pradesh	Rihand
37.	Sabarmati	Gujarat	Sabarmati
38.	Sharda Sahayak	U.P.	Ghagra
39.	Sone High Level Canal	Bihar	Sone
40.	Tawa	Madhya Pradesh	Tawa
41.	Tehri Dam	Uttarakhand	Bhagirathi
42.	Tungabhadra	Andhra Pradesh and Karnataka	Tungabhadra
43.	Ukai	Gujarat	Tapti
44.	Upper Krishna	Karnataka	Krishna
45.	Upper Penganga	Maharashtra	Penganga
46.	Uri Power Project	Jammu and Kashmir	Jhelum

General Knowledge

CLIMATE

- The climate of India may be described as tropical monsoon. On the basis of variations of monsoon the year is divided into four seasons.
  1. Winter Season (Mid December to Mid March).
  2. Summer Season (Mid March to May).
  3. Rainy Season (June to September).
  4. Retreating South-West Monsoon or North-East Monsoon (October to Mid December).

SOILS OF INDIA

- Soils is the layer of the earth surface made up of tiny rock debris and it is called 'soil'. In the soil, there are minerals, decomposed vegetation and bacteria.
- Indian soil has been divided into four categories, viz., Alluvial soil, Black soil, Red soil and Laterite soil. The Indian soil when compared with soil of any other country, is comparatively dry and requires an adquate supply of water for the purpose of cultivation.

☞ **Major Indian Crops**

Crops	Temp(°c)	Water(cm)	States where Produced
Wheat	15°-25°	60-90	Uttar Pradesh, Punjab, Haryana.
Rice	24°-26°	80-200	West Bengal, Uttar Pradesh, Andhra Pradesh, Bihar, Punjab
Maize	18°-21°	50-60	Uttar Pradesh, Maharashtra, Bihar
Jawar	20°-35°	40-60	Maharashtra, Madhya Pradesh, Karnataka
Soyabean	25°-27°	50-120	Madhya Pradesh
Cotton	20°-30°	80-150	Maharashtra, Gujarat, Karnataka, Madhya Pradesh
Tobacco	20°-25°	75-80	Andhra Pradesh, Gujarat, Karnataka, Maharashtra, Tamil Nadu, Bihar
Tea	24°-30°	100-200	Assam, West Bengal, Kerala, Tamil Nadu, Uttar Pradesh
Ground Nut	15°-25°	60-130	Gujarat, Maharashtra

☞ **Mineral Wealth at a Glance (Metallic Minerals)**

Mineral	Chief Producers
Bauxite	Odisha, Gujarat, Jharkhand
Chromite	Odisha, Karnataka
Coal	Jharkhand, West Bengal
Copper	Madhya Pradesh, Rajasthan
Diaspore	Uttar Pradesh, Madhya Pradesh
Gold	Karnataka
Iron	Odisha, Karnataka, Goa
Lead	Rajasthan, Andhra Pradesh
Lignite	Tamil Nadu
Manganese	Odisha, Karnataka
Natural Gas	Gujarat, Assam
Petroleum	Gujarat, Assam, Andhra Pradesh
Silver	Andhra Pradesh, Rajasthan, Jharkhand
Tungsten	Rajasthan
Zinc	Rajasthan, W. Bengal

TRANSPORT

RAILWAYS

Important Facts

- Indian Railways are the biggest national undertaking.
- The first Indian railway train rolled on its 34 km track from Bombay to Thane on April 16, 1853.
- Indian Railway System is fourth largest railway system in the world after America, China and Russia.
- The number of stations, till 31st March, 2017 is 7,349.
- As on 31st March, 2017 the total length of Indian railways is 67,368 km.
- Till 31st March, 2017 Indian railways have 11,461 locomotives, 53,453 passenger coaches, 6,714 other passenger trains coaches and 2,77,987 wagons.
- Rail Budget has been merged in Union Budget since 2017-18.
- The first electric train rolled on from Mumbai to Kurla on 3rd February, 1925.
- Kolkata Metro Rail is the first underground rail.
- The longest railway journey which takes 82.30 hours from Dibrugarh to Kanyakumari (4,286 km).
- The longest railway platform of the world is Gorakhpur. Its length is 1335.4 mtrs.
- The longest tunnel of Indian railways between Banihal and Gazigund stations in J&K is 11.21 km long.
- Indian Railway Board was established in 1905.
- Indian Railways have three gauges— Broad gauge, metre gauge and narrow gauge.
- Rapid metro train has been started in Gurugram (Haryana) on 14th November, 2013.
- Nehru Setu is the longest river railway bridge built on river Sone.

☞ **Zones and Headquarters of Indian Railways**

S.No.	Zone	Headquarters
1.	Central	Mumbai (Victoria Terminus)
2.	Eastern	Kolkata
3.	Northern	New Delhi
4.	North-Eastern	Gorakhpur
5.	North-East Frontier	Maligaon, Guwahati
6.	Southern	Chennai
7.	South-Central	Secunderabad
8.	South-Eastern	Kolkata
9.	Western	Mumbai, Churchgate
10.	East Coast	Bhubaneswar
11.	East Central	Hajipur
12.	North Central	Allahabad
13.	North Western	Jaipur
14.	South Western	Bangaluru (Hubli)
15.	West Central	Jabalpur
16.	South East Central	Bilaspur
17.	Kolkata Metro Railway	Kolkata

ROAD TRANSPORT

Important Facts

- The road network in India is one of the largest in the world. The total length of roads, at present is 56.17 lakh km.
- The total length of National Highways is 1,29,709 km.
- The Central Government owns the responsibility of 1,29,709 km long national highways.
- Border Road Organisation was established in 1960.
- Though the national highways do not constitute even 2 per cent of the total road length of the country, they bear about 40% of the traffic.

General Knowledge

- National Highways Development Project has been launched to link the four corners of the country by four or six lanes in a network. The four major cities—Kolkata, Delhi, Chennai and Mumbai will be linked by 5,882 km long roads in golden quadrilateral.
- Indian roads have been divided into three parts—(a) National Highways (b) State Highways (c) Border Roads.
- **NH44** is the longest highway of India.
- **NH47A** is the smallest highway of India.

☞ **Major National Highways**

N H	Connects
NH 1	New Delhi-Ambala-Jalandhar-Amritsar
NH 2	Delhi-Mathura-Agra-Kanpur-Allahabad-Varanasi-Kolkata
NH 3	Agra-Gwalior-Naski-Mumbai
NH 4	Thane and Chennai *via* Pune and Belgaum
NH 5	Kolkata-Chennai
NH 6	Kolkata-Dhule
NH 7	Varanasi-Kanyakumari (2369 km)
NH 8	Delhi-Mumbai (*via* Jaipur, Baroda and Ahmedabad)
NH 9	Mumbai-Vijaywada
NH 10	Delhi-Fazilka
NH 24	Delhi-Lucknow
NH 26	Lucknow-Varanasi

SHIPPING

Important Facts

- India has 7,516 km long coast line.
- Mumbai is the biggest port in the country. It is a natural harbour and handles more than one-fifth of the total traffic of the parts.
- The public sector company, The Shipping Corporation of India Limited was established on 2nd October, 1961.
- India has the largest merchant shipping fleet among the developing countries and ranks 16th in the world in shipping tonnage.
- There are 13 major ports in the country apart from about 200 minor ports. Major ports are under Central Government and others are maintained by State Governments.

Major Ports of Country

- 1. Kolkata, 2. Mumbai, 3. Nhava Sheva (J.L. Nehru Port), 4. Tuticorin, 5. Chennai, 6. Mormugao, 7. New Mangalore, 8. Paradeep, 9. Kandla, 10. Vishakhapatnam, 11. Cochin, 12. Haldia, 13. Ennore.

CIVIL AVIATION

- Air transport started in the country in 1911. JRD Tata was first person to take solo flight from Mumbai to Karachi in 1931. In 1953, according to Air-Corporation Act, all the civil aviation companies were nationalised and they came under two newformed corporations:

  1. Indian Airlines (Now Indian)

  2. Air India. Indian operates within the country and in neighbouring countries whereas Air India is the national carrier for external services. The headquarters of Air India are in Mumbai. Vayudoot was the third corporation which was established in 1983 but later on it was merged into Indian Airlines.

☞ **Major International Airports in India**

International Airports	City
Indira Gandhi International Airport	Delhi
Chennai International Airport	Chennai
Raja Sansi International Airport	Amritsar
Rajiv Gandhi International Airport	Hyderabad
Calicut International Airport	Calicut
Chhatrapati Shivaji International Airport	Mumbai
Bangalore International Airport	Bengaluru
Goa Airport in Vasco di Gama City	Goa
Netaji Subash Chandra Bose International Airport	Kolkata
Thriuvananthapuram International Airport	Thiruvananthapuram
Lokpriya Gopinath Bordoloi International Airport	Guwahati
Sardar Vallabhbhai Patel International Airport	Ahmedabad

Indian
POLITY

INDIAN CONSTITUTION

- Demand for a constituent Assembly composed of the people of India officially asserted by the Congress for the first time in 1935.
- The election for Indian Constitution Assembly held in 1946 according to the *Cabinet Mission Plan*.
- The first session of the Assembly was held in New Delhi on December 9, 1946. *Sachidanand Sinha* was elected provisional chairman of the session.
- On December 11, 1946, Dr. Rajendra Prasad was elected as the Permanent Chairman of the Constituent Assembly.
- The Constitution was framed by the Constituent Assembly of India, set-up in December 1946, in accordance with the Cabinet Mission Plan, under the Chairmanship of Sachidanand Sinha, initially.
- The total membership of Constituent Assembly was 299, when 70 were representatives from the Indian states and others from British India.
- The Chairman of the Drafting Committee was **Dr. BR Ambedkar**, also called the Father of the Constitution.
- The Constituent Assembly took 2 years, 11 months and 18 days to complete the Constitution.

- The Constitution, adopted on 8th November, 1949, contained 395 Articles and Schedules.
- The Constitution was delayed till 26th January because, in 1929, on this day Indian National Congress demanded Poorna Swaraj in Lahore Session under JL Nehru.
- Indian Constitution is a comprehensive document and it is the lengthiest written Constitution in the World.

THE PREAMBLE

- ***The Preamble of the Constitution:*** "We the people of India, having solemnly resolved to Constitute India into a Sovereign, Socialist, Secular Democratic Republic and to secure to all its citizen:
  Justice, Social, economic and political;
  Liberty of thought, expression, belief, faith and worship;
  Equality of status and of opportunity; and to promote among them all;
  Fraternity assuring the dignity of the individual and the unity and integrity of the nation;
  In our Constituent Assembly, this twenty-sixth day of November, 1949, do hereby adopt, enact and give to ourselves this constitution."

☞ Foreign Sources of Indian Constitution

Foreign Sources	Subject	Foreign Sources	Subject
Britain	Parliamentary system, collective responsibilities of Cabinet	Canada	Division of powers
America	Fundamental right, Citizenship, Independent Judiciary, Judicial review	Ireland	Directive principles
		Germany	Emergency provisions
		Russia	Fundamental duties
		Australia	Concurrent list

MAIN FEATURES

- It is perhaps the bulkiest written Constitution.
- It combines rigidity with flexibility.
- Envisages parliamentary system of government, both at the centre and the states, real executive, power with the council of Ministers.
- It provides a federal system of government with a unitary bias.
- It declares India a secular state.
- An elaborate list of Fundamental Rights and Duties is given in the Constitution.
- It lays down Directive Principles of State Policy. It provides for single citizenship.
- It makes special provision for the protection of backward classes.
- It grants rights to vote to all adults above the age of 18 years without any distinction.

IMPORTANT ARTICLES

PART - I

UNION AND ITS TERRITORIES
(ARTICLE 1 - 4)

- The Constitution says, "India, that is Bharat, shall be a Union of States".
- Parliament has the power to create any State, reduce it, change the name of boundaries of any State.

PART - II

CITIZENSHIP (ARTICLE 5 - 11)

- The Constitution provides for a single Citizenship.

- *Indian Citizenship can be acquire:*
  1. by birth
  2. by descent
  3. by registration
  4. by naturalisation
  5. by incorporation of territory
- *Indian Citizenship can be lost by:*
  1. renunciation;
  2. termination — it takes place if a citizen of India voluntary acquires the citizenship of another country; and
  3. deprivation — if the Government terminates the citizenship.

PART - III

FUNDAMENTAL RIGHTS
(ARTICLE 12 - 35)

- Following fundamental rights are enjoyed by every Indian citizen, irrespective of caste, colour, creed and sex:
  1. *Right to Equality:* No special privileges, no distinction on grounds of religion, caste, creed and sex.
  2. *Right to Freedom:* The right to freedom of expression and speech, the right to choose one's own profession, the right to reside in any part of the Indian Union.
  3. *Right to Freedom to Religion:* Except when it is in the interest of public order, morality, health or other conditions, everybody has the right to profess, practice and propagate his religion freely.

4. ***Cultural and Educational Rights:*** The Constitution provides that every community can run its own institutions to preserve its own culture and language.
5. ***Right against Exploitation:*** Traffic in human beings and forced labour and the employment of children under 14 years in factories or mines, are punishable offences.
6. ***Rights to Constitutional Remedies:*** When a citizen finds that any of his fundamental rights has been encroached upon, he can move the Supreme Court, which has been empowered to safeguard the fundamental rights of a citizen (Article 32).

PART - IV

DIRECTIVE PRINCIPLES OF STATE POLICY (ARTICLE 36 - 51)

- Directive principles are not enforceable through courts. Main aim of Directive principles is to provide social and economic base of a genuine democracy.

Some Important Directive Principles:

- Provisions for adequate means of livelihood for all citizens (Art. 39).
- Right to work (Art. 41).
- Right to human condition of work and maternity relief (Art. 42).
- Right to a living wage and condition of work ensuring decent standard of life of worker (Art. 43).
- Common Civil Code (Art. 44).
- Prohibit consumption of liquor (Art. 47).
- Prevent slaughter of useful cattle (Art. 48).
- Organise Panchayati Raj (Art. 40).
- Separate the judiciary from the executive (Art. 50).
- Protect and maintain places of historic monuments (Art. 49).
- International peace (Art. 51).

PART - IV A

FUNDAMENTAL DUTIES (ARTICLE 51A)

- The fundamental duties for the Indian citizens have been incorporated in the Constitution through the Constitution (42nd) Amendment Act, 1976. These duties are:
  1. to abide by the Constitution and respect its ideals and institutions, the National Flag and the National Anthem;
  2. to cherish and follow the noble deeds which inspired our national struggle for freedom;
  3. to uphold and protect the sovereignty, unity and integrity of India;
  4. to defend the country and render national service when called upon to do so;
  5. to promote harmony and the spirit of common brotherhood amongst all the people transcending religious, regional or sectional diversities and to renounce practices derogatory to the dignity of women;
  6. to value and preserve the rich heritage of our composite culture;
  7. to protect and improve natural environment including forests, lakes, rivers and wildlife, and to have compassion for living creatures;
  8. to develop the scientific temper, humanism and the spirit of inquiry and reform;
  9. to safeguard public property and to abjure violence;
  10. to strive towards excellence in all spheres of individual and collective activity so that the nation constantly rises to higher levels of endeavour and achievement.
  11. who is parent or guardian to provide opportunities for education to his child or, as the case may be, ward between age of six and fourteen years.

General Knowledge

PART - V

UNION (ARTICLE 52 - 151)

THE PRESIDENT

- The President is the Constitutional head of the Republic of India. He is more or less the titular head of the executive.

- He is the constitutional head but not the real executive. The real power is vested in the hands of the Council of Ministers.

- President is the first citizen of India.

- **Qualifications:** (i) Indian citizen, (ii) age not less than 35 years, (iii) should have qualification for election to Lok Sabha, (iv) should not hold any office of profit, (v) should not be a Member of Parliament or State Legislature.

- **Election:** Indirectly elected through Electoral College consisting of elected members of both the Houses of the Parliament and elected members of the Legislative Assemblies of the States.

- According to the 70th Amendment Act, 1992, the expression 'States' include the National Capital Territory of Delhi and the Union Territory of Puducherry. Members of the Legislative Councils have no right to vote in the Presidential election.

- **Powers:** He makes appointments to all the constitutional posts.

- He can address either House of Parliament and dissolve Lok Sabha.

- All Bills passed by Parliament must receive his assent to become an Act.

- He issues ordinances when Parliament is not in session. No Money Bill can be introduced in Lok Sabha without his recommendation.

- He appoints 12 members of special repute in the Rajya Sabha and 2 members in the Lok Sabha of the Anglo-Indian Community.

- He has the power of *Pardon* to a criminal in special cases.

- The President holds the office for a period of five years. He is eligible for re-election.

- He draws the salary of ₹ 5.0 lakh per month with various allowances.

- He is also entitled to rent free official residence called Rashtrapati Bhawan.

VICE-PRESIDENT

- **Article 63** of the Constitution stipulates a Vice-President for India.

- The Vice-President acts as the ex-officio Chairman of the Council of States (Rajya Sabha).

- He is elected by an electoral college consisting of the members of both Houses of Parliament in accordance with the system of proportional representation by means of the single transferable vote. He must be a citizen of India, not less than 35 years of age, and should be eligible for election as a member of the Council of States.

- Disputes in connection with election of a president or a vice-president are to be a dealt with in accordance with Article-71. Such disputes shall be decided by the Supreme Court.

- Present salary of the Vice-President is ₹ 4.0 lakh per month.

COUNCIL OF MINISTERS

- The Constitution of India provides for a parliament system of government under which the President is only Constitutional ruler and the real power is exercised by the Council of Ministers, headed by the Prime Minister.

- Council of Ministers is composed of all Union Ministers—the Prime Minister, Cabinet Ministers, Ministers of State and Deputy Ministers.

- The Council of Ministers is Collectively responsible to the Lok Sabha.

- The Prime Minister is a link between the President and the Council of Ministers.

Prime Minister

- The Prime Minister is the leader of the majority party in the Parliament.
- He is appointed by the President. Other Ministers are appointed by the president on his advice.
- The Prime Minister is the head of the Government and the head of the Council of Ministers.
- Jawaharlal Nehru was the first Prime Minister and the longest serving so far.

Union Legislature

- The Legislature of the Union, which is called 'Parliament' Consists of the President and the two Houses of Parliament known as the Council of states (Rajya Sabha) and the House of the People (Lok Sabha).

RAJYA SABHA

- The Rajya Sabha is the Upper House of the Parliament and it is constituted of representatives from the States or the Constituent units of the Indian Union.
- It is a permanent body, one third of its members retiring after every two years.
- Its maximum strength is 250. Out of these, twelve members are nominated by the President from well-known personalities in the realm of Science, Art, Literature and Social Service. Rest of 238 representatives of the States and Union Territories are elected.
- Currently, the strength of the Rajya Sabha is 245.

LOK SABHA

- The Lok Sabha whose life is five years, is the Lower House of Parliament and comprises of members directly elected by the people.
- The House of the people (Lok Sabha) at present consists of 545 members of these, 530 members are directly elected from the states and 13 from Union Territories while 2 are nominated by the President from Anglo-Indian community.

- The House of the People shall continue for five years (unless sooner dissolved) from the date of its meeting and no longer and the expiry of the said period of 5 years shall operate as dissolution of the House.

Parliamentary Committees

- There are several Parliamentary Committees to assist the Parliament in its deliberations.
- These are appointed or elected by the respective Houses of Lok Sabha and Rajya Sabha on a motion made or are nominated by their presiding officers.
- Among the Standing Committees, three are financial Committees: (i) Public Account Committee; (ii) Estimate Committee; (iii) Public undertaking Committee.

Speaker of Lok Sabha

- Speaker is elected by the Lok Sabha from among its members.
- The Speaker will have the final power to maintain order within the House of the People and to interpret its rules of procedure.
- A Deputy-Speaker is also elected to officiate in absence of the Speaker.
- *G.V. Mavlankar* was the first Speaker of the Lok Sabha (1952-1956).

Supreme Court

- The Constitution provides for the Supreme Court, which consists of Chief Justice and 30 judges. They are appointed by the President of India.

Qualification and Tenure

- Eligibility conditions for a judge of the Supreme Court are that he must be : (i) a citizen of India; (ii) a judge of a high court for a minimum period of 5 years; or (iii) an advocate of a high court for at least ten years or a distinguished jurist.
- Judges hold office till the age of 65.

General Knowledge

- They can resign earlier or can be removed by the President on the recommendation of the two Houses of the Parliament by 2/3rd majority of the members present and voting.

Powers

- *Original jurisdiction:* Cases involving Government of India and the states or cases involving the enforcement of Fundamental Rights fall under original jurisdiction.
- *Appellate Jurisdiction:* In cases which are brought to it in the form of appeals against the judgement of the lower courts—It hears appeals in civil and criminal cases.
- *Advisory functions:* the Supreme Court advises the President on the constitutionality of a particular legal matter. However, its advice is not binding on the President. ***Other Powers:***
  1. it is a court of record and can punish for contempt of itself;
  2. it can make rules for regulating the practice and procedure of courts with the approval of the President; and
  3. it can recommend to the President the removal of chairman and members of the UPSC. Supreme Court enjoys the power of judicial review (right of the court which declares as unconstitutional, the laws passed by the legislature and orders issued by executive) though it is not specifically mentioned in the Constitution.
- The first Chief Justice of India was H.J. Kania (1950-51).

COMPTROLLER AND AUDITOR GENERAL (CAG) (ARTICLE 148-151)

- The Comptroller and Auditor General of India is guardian of the public purse.
- It is his duty to see that not a *paisa* is spent out of consolidated fund of India or of a state without the authority of the appropriate legislature.

- He is appointed by President of India.
- A person with long administrative experience and knowledge of accounts is appointed.
- Holds office for 6 yrs or till 65 yrs of age.
- The President can remove him only on the recommendation of the 2 houses of Parliament (as in case of judge of Supreme Court).
- The CAG submits its reports to the President (in case of accounts relating to the Union Government) or to the State Governors (for State Government Accounts).
- The first CAG of India was *V Narahari Rao* (1948-1954).
- The CAG is not eligible for further office under the Union or State Governments. The expenses of the office of the CAG is charged to the Consolidated Fund of India.

ATTORNEY GENERAL OF INDIA

- The Attorney General of India is the first law officer of the Government of India.
- Though he is not a member of cabinet he has the right to speak in the House of Parliament, but he has no right to vote.
- The Attorney General of India shall be appointed by the President and shall hold office during his pleasure.
- His duty shall be to give advice on such legal matter from time-to-time as may be referred to him by the President.
- To be appointed as Attorney General, a candidate must be qualified to be appointed as a Judge of the Supreme Court.
- The Attorney General can participate in proceedings of the Parliament without the Right to Vote (Article 88).
- The first Attorney General of Independent India was MC Setalvad (1950-1963).

PART - VI

THE STATES (ARTICLE 152 - 237)

THE GOVERNOR

- The Governor is appointed by the President and holds office during the pleasure of the President.
- Apart from the power to appoint the council of ministers, if the governor finds that the government of state cannot be carried on in accordance with the provisions of the constitution (Art. 356), he may send his report to the President who may assume to himself the functions of the government of the state. (This is popularly known as 'President's Rule').
- Article 161 gives the Governor the power to grant pardons, reprieves, remission of punishment to persons convicted under the state law.
- Article 171 states that the States where Legislative Councils exists, the Governor can nominate some members from amongst those distinguished in literature, science, arts, cooperative movement and social service.

STATES LEGISLATURE
(ARTICLE 168 - 212)

- The state legislature consists of Governor and legislative assembly.
- In some state like *Bihar, Maharashtra, Andhra Pradesh, Karnataka, Uttar Pradesh, Telangana and Jammu* and *Kashmir* have a legislative council.
- The membership of the council should not be more than *one-third* of the legislative assembly but not less than 40.
- The legislative assembly of each state shall be composed of members chosen by direct election on the basis of adult suffrage and the number of members shall not be more than 500 or less than 60.
- The assembly of Sikkim, Goa, Puducherry and Mizoram have less than 60 members.

HIGH COURTS (ARTICLE 214-232)

- The High Court stands at the apex of the State Judiciary.
- As per the Constitution, there shall be a High Court in each State. But there may be a common High Court for two or more States and Union Territory, if it is provided by a law of the Parliament. For example, the Chennai High Court has its Jurisdiction over the State of Tamil Nadu and the Union Territory of Puducherry.
- The State Government has no control over it.
- There are 25 High Courts in India.
- The Calcutta High Court, established in 1862, is the oldest High Court in India.

THE PANCHAYATS (ARTICLE 243-243 O)

- Panchayati Raj was introduced in India with a view to associated the people with administration at grass-root level.
- It is a three-tier system as recommended by Balwant Rai Mehta Committee.
- Introduced by the 73rd Amendment Act, 1992 which envisaged a three tier system of local governance.
  These are:
  1. Gram Panchayat at the village level
  2. Panchayat Samiti at the block level
  3. Zila Parishad at the district level.

THE MUNICIPALITIES
(ARTICLE 243 P-243 ZG)

- Big cities have municipal corporations headed by the elected Mayor.
- For small towns there are elected boards or councils, in turn, elect their Presidents.
- Introduced by the 74th Amendment Act, 1993 which envisages three types of urban local bodies, namely, municipality (nagar palika), city council (nagar panchayat).
- Municipal governance in India was first introduced in Madras in 1688.

General Knowledge 

☞ Jurisdiction and Seat of High Courts

Name	Year	Territorial Jurisdiction	Seat
Allahabad	1866	Uttar Pradesh	Allahabad (Bench at Lucknow)
Andhra Pradesh	2019	Andhra Pradesh	Amravati
Bombay	1862	Maharashtra, Goa, Dadar and Nagar Haveli and Daman and Diu	Mumbai (Benches at Nagpur, Panaji and Aurangabad)
Calcutta	1862	West Bengal and Andaman & Nicobar	Kolkata (Circuit Bench at Port Blair)
Chhattisgarh	2000	Chhattisgarh	Bilaspur
Delhi	1966	Delhi	Delhi
Guwahati	1948	Assam, Nagaland, Mizoram and Arunachal Pradesh	Guwahati (Benches at Kohima, Aizawl and Itanagar)
Gujarat	1960	Gujarat	Ahmedabad
Himachal Pradesh	1971	Himachal Pradesh	Shimla
Jammu & Kashmir	1928	Jammu & Kashmir	Srinagar and Jammu
Jharkhand	2000	Jharkhand	Ranchi
Karnataka	1884	Karnataka	Bengaluru (Circuit Benches at Dharwar and Gulbarga)
Kerala	1958	Kerala & Lakshadweep	Ernakulam
Madhya Pradesh	1956	Madhya Pradesh	Jabalpur (Benches at Gwalior and Indore)
Madras	1862	Tamil Nadu & Puducherry	Chennai (Bench at Madurai)
Orissa	1948	Odisha	Cuttack
Patna	1916	Bihar	Patna
Punjab and Haryana	1966	Punjab, Haryana and Chandigarh	Chandigarh
Rajasthan	1949	Rajasthan	Jodhpur (Bench at Jaipur)
Sikkim	1975	Sikkim	Gangtok
Uttarakhand	2000	Uttarakhand	Nainital
Tripura	2013	Tripura	Agartala
Meghalaya	2013	Meghalaya	Shillong
Manipur	2013	Manipur	Imphal
Telangana	2019	Telangana	Hyderabad

PART - XIII

(ARTICLE 301 - 307)

- In this part from Article 301-307 trade, commerce and intercourse within the territory of India are given.

PART - XIV

(ARTICLE 308 - 323)

- In this part services under the union and the states are given.
- *Article 312:* All India Services and *Article 315:* Public Service Commissions for the Union and for the States.

- The first Public Service Commission was set up in 1926, on the recommendations of the Lee Commission.

UNION PUBLIC SERVICE COMMISSION (UPSC)

- This Commission is responsible for:
  1. recruitment to all civil services and posts, under the Union Government by written examinations, interviews and promotions, and
  2. advising the Government on all matters relating to methods of recruitment, principles to be followed

in making promotions and transfers. Its Chairman is appointed by the President.

STAFF SELECTION COMMISSION (SSC)

- The Union Government has constituted a Staff Selection Commission for recruitment to non-technical Class III posts in the central government and in subordinate offices.
- The Administrative Reforms Commission had recommended the setting up of such a Commission.
- The Commission has also been entrusted with the responsibility of making recruitment to Group 'B' services like Assistants' and Stenographers Grade 'C'.
- The Commission has a chairman and two members.

ELECTIONS (ARTICLE 324-329)

- The Constitution provides for an independent election commission to ensure free and fair election to the Parliament, the State legislature and the offices of President and Vice-President.
- Consists of Chief Election Commissioner +2 Election Commissioners. They all enjoy equal powers.
- The Chief Election Commissioner and other Election Commissioners are appointed by the President.
- Election Commissioners are appointed for a term of 5 yrs.
- They are not eligible for re-appointment. Also, they cannot hold any office of profit after their retirement.
- The Election Commission was established on 25th January, 1950 under Article 324 of the Constitution.
- The first Chief Election Commissioner was *Sukumar Sen.*

Functions

- Preparation of electoral rolls and keeping voters list updated.
- Recognition of various political parties and allotment of election symbols.

NITI AAYOG

- The NITI Aayog replaced Planning Commission on January 1, 2015 is an advisory body engaged in the task of meaningful national planning.
- It is neither constitutional nor statutory.
- The Prime Minister is the Chairman of the Aayog.

Functions

- The functions of the NITI Aayog are:
    1. The Aayog will recommend a national agenda, including strategic and technical advice on elements of policy and economic matters.
    2. It will also develop mechanisms for village level plans and aggregate these progressively at higher levels of government.
    3. The Aayog will work towards fostering co-operative federalism for providing a national agenda to the Centre and States.

NATIONAL DEVELOPMENT COUNCIL

- The National Development Council, set-up in 1952, consists of representatives of the Central Government as well as the State governments.
- It is the supreme body insofar as planning is concerned and it determines policies, issues guidelines, reviews working of the plan and finally approves the plan.
- The Council consists of the Prime Minister (Chairman), all Union Cabinet Ministers, Chief Ministers of all States and Union Territories and the Vice-Chairman and members of the NITI Aayog.
- For matters relating to Plans and planning, the Union Minister of Planning is responsible to the Parliament.

General Knowledge 

FINANCE COMMISSION

- The constitution of the Finance Commission is laid down in Art. 280.
- The chairman must be a person having experience in public affairs; and the other four members also having wide experience in financial matters.
- It consists of Chairman and 4 other members.
- It shall be the duty of the Finance Commission to advice the President on matters such as the distribution between the Union and states of the net proceeds of taxes that is required to be shared.
- The Finance Commission is not a permanent body. It is dissolved after it has submitted its recommendations.

☞ Important Amendments to the Constitution

First Amendment, 1951: Added Ninth Schedule.

Twenty-second Amendment, 1969: Formation of Meghalaya within the state of Assam was facilitated.

Twenty-sixth Amendment, 1971: The privy and privileges of the former rulers of Indian States were abolished.

Thirty-first Amendment, 1973: The upper limit of representation of states was raised from 500 to 525. The upper limit for representation of the UTs was reduced from 25 to 20.

Thirty-sixth Amendment, 1975: Sikkim was made a full-fledged state of Indian Union and it was included in the First Schedule.

Thirty-eight Amendment, 1975: This act led to the amendment of Article 123, Article 213 and Article 352 which stated that the satisfaction of President or of Governor contained in these Articles would be called in question in any court of law.

Forty-second Amendment, 1976: This amendment was done in accordance with the recommendations of Swaran Singh Committee and included a number of amendments.

Forty-third Amendment, 1977: It provided for the restoration of the Jurisdiction of the Supreme Court and High Courts, curtailed by the enactment of the Constitution (Forty-Second Amendment) Act, 1976.

Forty-fourth Amendment, 1978: The right to property was deleted as Fundamental Right and was made a legal right.

Fifty-third Amendment, 1986: The Act grants statehood to the Union Territory of Mizoram, thus making it the 23rd State of the Indian Unions.

Fifty-sixth Amendment, 1987: The UT of Goa Converted into Goa state through this amendment whereas Daman and Diu were organised under a new UT.

Seventy-third Amendment, 1992: It is concerning Panchayati Raj.

Seventy-fourth Amendment, 1992: It is regarding Municipal Boards and Corporations.

Ninety-first Amendment, 2003: It is regarding restricting the total number of Ministers including Prime Minister/Chief Minister in Lok Sabha and State Legislatures to 15% of the total number of the Union or State Legislatures.

Ninety-sixth Amendment, 2011: Amendment of 8th Schedule, it replaces 'Orissa' with 'Odisha'.

One-Hundredth Amendment, 2015: Amended the first schedule for the purpose of exchange of enclaves, in pursuance of the Agreement between India and Bangladesh.

One Hundred and First Amendment, 2016: The act amends the constitution to introduce "The Goods and Services Tax (GST)". The act also provided for compensation to States for loss of revenue on account of introduction of goods and services tax.

 **General Knowledge**

NATIONAL SYMBOLS

NATIONAL EMBLEM

- State emblem of India is an adaptation from the Sarnath Lion Capital of Ashoka. It was adopted by the Government of India on January 26, 1950. In the adapted form, only three lions are visible, the fourth being hidden from the view.
- The wheel (Dharma Chakra) appears in relief in the centre of the abacus with a bull on the right and a horse on the left.
- The bell-shaped lotus has been omitted. The words "Satyameva Jayate" meaning "Truth alone triumphs" are inscribed below the Emblem in Devanagari script.

NATIONAL FLAG

- The National Flag of India is a horizontal tricolour of deep saffron (Kesari), white and dark green in equal proportion.
- In the centre of the white band there is a wheel in navy blue colour. It has 24 spokes.
- The ratio of the length and the breadth of the flag is 3 : 2. Its design was adopted by the Constituent Assembly of India on July 22, 1947.

NATIONAL ANTHEM

- Rabindranath Tagore's song 'Jana-gana-mana' was adopted by the Constituent Assembly as the National Anthem of India on January 24, 1950.

Jana-gan-mana-adhinayaka jaya he, Bharata-bhagya-vidhata
Punjab-Sindh-Gujarat-Maratha-Dravida-Utkala-Banga
Vindhya-Himachala-Yamuna-Ganga Uchhala-jaladhi-taranga.
Tava subha name jage, Tava subha asisa mange, Gahe tava jaya gatha,
Jana-gana-mangala-dayak, jaya he Bharata bhagya vidhata,
Jaya he, jaya he, jaya he, Jaya jaya jaya, jaya he.

NATIONAL SONG

- Bankim Chandra Chatterji's 'Vande Mataram' which was a source of inspiration to the people in their struggle for freedom, has been adopted as National Song. It has an equal status with the National Anthem.

Vande Mataram
Sujalam, suphalam, malayaja-shitalam,
Shasya shyamalam, Mataram
Shubhrajyotsna, pulkita yaminim,
Phulla kusumita drumadalashobhinim,
Subhasinim sumadhura—bhashinim,
Sukhadam, Varadam, Mataram.

- **National Bird and Animal of India:** Peacock and Tiger; **National Aquatic Animal:** Dolphin; **National Flower:** Lotus; **National Game:** Hockey; **National Calendar:** It was adopted on March 22, 1957. It has 365 days in the year and the first month of the year is Chaitra.

Months of the National

Calendar: (1) Chaitra, (2) Vaishakha, (3) Jaishtha, (4) Ashadha, (5) Shravan, (6) Bhadra, (7) Ashvina, (8) Kartika, (9) Marga-Shirsha, (10) Pausha, (11) Magha, (12) Phalguna.

Indian ECONOMY

NATIONAL INCOME

- National income is a flow concept not a stock concept.
- In India, National income estimates are related with the financial year (April 1 to 31st March).
  1. **GNP (Gross National Product):** GNP refers to the money value of total output or production of final goods and services produced by the nationals of a country during a given period of time, generally a year.
  2. **NNP (Net National Product):** NNP is obtained by subtracting depreciation value from GNP. NNP can be calculated in two ways: (a) at market prices of goods and services and (b) at factor cost.
  3. **National Income:** When NNP is obtained at factor cost, it is known as National Income. National Income is calculated by subtracting net indirect taxes from NNP at market prices. The obtained value is known as NNP at factor cost or National income.
  4. **Personal Income:** Personal income is that income which is actually obtained by nationals. Personal income is obtained by subtracting corporate taxes and payments made for social securities provisions from national income and adding to it government transfer payments, business transfer payments and net interest paid by the government.

- For measuring national income in India, in 1868, the first attempt was made by *Dada Bhai Nauroji*. He, in his book, *"Poverty and Un-British Rule in India"*, estimated Indian per capita annual income at a level of ₹ 20.
- After independence, the Government of India appointed the National Income Committee in August, 1949, under the Chairmanship of Prof. P.C. Mahalanobies, to compile authoritative estimates of national income.
- National income includes the contribution of three sectors—Primary sector, Secondary sector, Tertiary sector.
- Under Primary Sector—Agriculture, Forest, Fisheries and allied sector are included.
- Under Secondary Sector—Manufacturing, Construction, Electricity, Gas and Water Supply are included.
- Under Teritiary Sector—Trade, Transport, Communication, Banking, Insurance, Real Estate, Community and Personal Services are included.
- At present estimation of national income is based on the base year of 2011-12.

POPULATION

- Every year 11th July is celebrated as the World Population Day.
- The first census of India was done in 1872 during the reign of Viceroy Lord Mayo. But a series of census (After every ten years) was adopted in 1881 during the reign of Viceroy Lord Ripon.
- 2011 census is the 15th census of India, and the 7th census of free India.

☞ **2011 Census Highlights**

- *Population of India*—Total Indian population is 17.7% of total world population—1,21,08,54,977 (Male: 62,32,70,258; Female: 58,75,84,719)
- *Decadal Growth (2001-2011)*—17.7 per cent (Males: 17.1 per cent; Females: 18.3 per cent)
- *Hightest Decadal Growth (State-wise)*—Meghalaya (27.9 per cent)
- *Lowest Decadal Growth (State-wise)*—Nagaland (–0.6 per cent)
- *Most populous State*—Uttar Pradesh (16.17 per cent of National Population)
- *Density of population*—382 persons per sq. km.
- *Most densly populated State*—Bihar : 1106 per sq. km
- *Sex Ratio*—943 females per 1000 males
- *Total Literacy Rate*—73% (Males – 80.9%) (Females – 64.06%)
- *Highest Literacy (State-wise)*—Kerala (94%)
- *Lowest Literacy (State-wise)*—Bihar (61.8)

☞ **Other Details**

(a) Population of India

1951	36,10,88,090	1961	43,92,34,771
1971	54,81,59,652	1981	68,33,29,097
1991	84,64,21,039	2001	102,87,37,436
2011	1,21,08,54,977		

(b) Density of Population (Persons per square kilometre)

1951	113	1961	138
1971	177	1981	216
1991	267	2001	324
2011	382		

(c) Annual Compound Rate of Growth

1941-1951	1.25 per cent
1951-1961	1.96 per cent
1961-1971	2.22 per cent
1971-1981	2.20 per cent
1981-1991	2.14 per cent
1991-2001	1.95 per cent
2001-2011	1.64 per cent

POVERTY

- Poverty can be defined as a social phenomenon in which a section of society is unable to fulfil even the basic necessities of life.
- In India, the generally accepted definition of poverty emphasises minimum level of living rather than a reasonable level of living.
- An expert group of planning commission, defined poverty line on a nutritional norm of per capita daily intake of 2400 calories in rural areas and 2100 calories for urban areas. A person who fails to obtain this minimum level of calories is treated as being below the poverty line.
- There are two types of common standards in economic literature for the measurement of poverty:
  1. *Absolute Poverty:* In the absolute standard, minimum physical quantities of cereals, pulses, milk, butter, etc. are determined for a subsistence level and then the price quotations converted into monetary terms the physical quantities.
  2. *Relative Standard:* According to the relative standard, income distribution of the population in different fractile

General Knowledge

2011 CENSUS OF INDIA : POPULATION DISTRIBUTION, POPULATION DENSITY AND LITERACY RATE

S. No.	State/ Union Territories*	Population 2011			Population Density (per sq. km.)	Literacy Rate 2011		
		Persons	Males	Females	2011	Persons	Males	Females
	INDIA	1,21,08,54,977	62,32,70,258	58,75,34,719	382	73.0	80.9	64.6
1.	Jammu and Kashmir	1,25,41,302	66,40,662	59,00,640	124	67.2	76.8	56.4
2.	Himachal Pradesh	68,64,602	34,81,873	33,82,729	123	82.8	89.5	75.9
3.	Punjab	2,77,43,338	1,46,39,465	1,31,03,873	551	75.8	80.4	70.7
4.	Chandigarh	10,55,450	5,80,663	4,74,787	9,258	86.0	90.0	81.2
5.	Uttarakhand	1,00,86,292	51,37,773	49,48,519	189	78.8	87.4	70.0
6.	Haryana	2,53,51,462	1,34,94,734	1,18,56,728	573	75.6	84.1	65.9
7.	Delhi	1,67,87,941	89,87,326	78,00,615	11,320	86.2	90.9	80.8
8.	Rajasthan	6,85,48,437	3,55,50,997	3,29,97,440	200	66.1	79.2	52.1
9.	Uttar Pradesh	19,98,12,341	10,44,80,510	9,53,31,831	829	67.7	77.3	57.2
10.	Bihar	10,40,99,452	5,42,78,157	4,98,21,295	1,106	61.8	71.2	51.5
11.	Sikkim	6,10,577	3,23,070	2,87,507	86	81.4	86.6	75.6
12.	Arunachal Pradesh	13,83,727	7,13,912	6,69,815	17	65.4	72.6	57.7
13.	Nagaland	19,78,502	10,24,649	9,53,853	119	79.6	82.8	76.1
14.	Manipur	28,55,794	14,38,586	14,17,208	128	76.9	83.5	70.2
15.	Mizoram	10,97,206	5,55,339	5,41,867	52	91.3	93.3	89.3
16.	Tripura	36,73,917	18,74,376	17,99,541	350	87.2	91.5	82.7
17.	Meghalya	29,66,889	14,91,832	14,75,057	132	74.4	76.0	72.9
18.	Assam	3,12,05,576	1,59,39,443	1,52,66,133	398	72.2	77.8	66.3
19.	West Bengal	9,12,76,115	4,68,09,027	4,44,67,088	1,028	76.3	81.7	70.5
20.	Jharkhand	3,29,88,134	1,69,30,315	1,60,57,819	414	66.4	76.8	55.4
21.	Odisha	4,19,74,218	2,12,12,136	2,07,62,082	270	72.9	81.6	64.0
22.	Chhattisgarh	2,55,45,198	1,28,32,895	1,27,12,303	189	70.3	80.3	60.2
23.	Madhya Pradesh	7,26,26,809	3,76,12,306	3,50,14,503	236	69.3	78.7	59.2
24.	Gujarat	6,04,39,692	3,14,91,260	2,89,48,432	308	78.0	85.8	69.7
25.	Daman and Diu	2,43,247	1,50,301	92,946	2,191	87.1	91.5	79.5
26.	Dadra & Nagar Haweli	3,43,709	1,93,760	1,49,949	700	76.2	85.2	64.3
27.	Maharashtra	11,23,74,333	5,82,43,056	5,41,31,277	365	82.3	88.4	75.9
28.	Andhra Pradesh	4,93,86,799	2,47,38,068	2,46,48,731	308	67.4	74.8	60.0
29.	Karnataka	6,10,95,297	3,09,66,657	3,01,28,640	319	75.4	82.5	68.1
30.	Goa	14,58,545	7,39,140	7,19,405	394	88.7	92.6	84.7
31.	Lakshadweep	64,473	33,123	31,350	2,149	91.8	95.6	87.9
32.	Kerala	3,34,06,061	1,60,27,412	1,73,78,649	860	94.0	96.1	92.1
33.	Tamil Nadu	7,21,47,030	3,61,37,975	3,60,09,055	555	80.1	86.8	73.4
34.	Puducherry	12,47,953	6,12,511	6,35,442	2,547	85.8	91.3	80.7
35.	Andaman & Nicobar Island	3,80,581	2,02,871	1,77,710	46	86.6	90.3	82.4
36.	Telangana	3,51,93,978	17,704,078	17,489,900	308	66.5	75.0	57.9

groups is estimated and a comparison of the levels of living of the top 5 to 10 per cent with the bottom 5 to 10 per cent of the population reflects the relative standards of poverty.

- As per the Tendulkar Committee Report, the national poverty line at 2004-05 prices was a monthly per capita consumption expenditure of ₹ 446.68 in rural and ₹ 578.80 in urban areas in 2004-05.

☞ **Poverty Ratios (per cent)**

	Earlier estimates (URP) based on the Lakdawala methodology		Estimates (MRP) based on the Tendulkar methodology	
	1993-1994	2004-2005	1993-1994	2004-2005
Rural	37.3	28.3	50.1	41.8
Urban	32.4	25.7	31.8	25.7
Total	36.0	27.5	45.3	37.2

☞ **Various Employment Generations Programmes**

Programme	Year of beginning
Community Development Programme (CDP)	1952
Intensive Agriculture Development Programme (IADP)	1960-61
Drought-Prone Area Programme (DPAP)	1973
Command Area Development Programme (CADP)	1974-75
Food for Work Programme	1977-78
Antyodaya Yojana	1977-78
Training Rural Youth for Self-Employment (TRYSEM)	Aug. 15, 1979
Integrated Rural Development Programme (IRDP)	Oct. 2, 1980
National Rural Employment Programme (NREP)	1980
Development of Women and Children in Rural Areas (DWCRA)	Sept. 1982
Rural Landless Employment Guarantee Programme (RLEGP)	Aug. 15, 1983
Self-Employment to the Educated Unemployed Youth (SEEUY)	1983-84
National Fund for Rural Development (NFRD)	February 1984
Council for Advancement of People's Action and Rural Technology (CAPART)	Sept. 1, 1986
Self-Employment Programme for the Urban Poor (SEPUP)	Sept. 1986
Jawahar Rozgar Yojana	April 1989
Nehru Rozgar Yojana	Oct. 1989
Scheme of Urban Wage Employment (SUWE)	1990
Employment Assurance Scheme (EAS)	Oct. 2, 1993
Prime Minister's Integrated Urban Poverty Eradication Programme (PMIUPEP)	Nov. 18, 1995
Swarna Jayanti Shahari Rozgar Yojana (SJSRY)	Dec. 1997
Swarna Jayanti Gram Swarozgar Yojana	April 1999 Yojana
Mahatma Gandhi National Rural Employment Guarantee Act (MNREGA)	Feb. 2, 2006

AGRICULTURE

- Agriculture is an important sector of the economy. Though the share of agriculture in national income has come down since the inception of planning era in the economy but still it has substantial share in GDP.
- Agriculture Contributes about 15 per cent of gross domestic product.

General Knowledge 

- Agriculture accounted for about 52 per cent employment in the country.
- Agriculture provides raw materials to various industries and other agro-based industries. Cotton and Jute textile industries, Sugar, Vanaspati industry etc. are directly dependent on agriculture.
- India's foreign trade is deeply associated with Agriculture Sector. Agriculture and Allied Sector Accounts for 12.1% of the total exports during 2014-15 against 6.9% of 2010-11. Agri exports (including marine) grew by 5.82% in 2014-15.

LAND REFORM PROGRAMMES

- Land reform programme in India include:
  1. Elimination of intermediaries.
  2. Tenancy Reform.
  3. Determination of ceiling of holding per family and to distribute surplus land among landless people.
  4. Consolidation of holdings.

IRRIGATION

- The planning commission has introduced a new classification of irrigation schemes:
  1. *Major Irrigation Schemes*—Those with culturable command areas (CCA) more than 10,000 hectares.
  2. *Medium Irrigation Schemes*—Those with culturable command areas (CCA) between 2,000 to 10,000 hectares.
  3. *Minor Irrigation Scheme*—Those with culturable command area (CCA) upto 2,000 hectares.
- *Micro Irrigation:* A centrally sponsored scheme on Micro Irrigation (MI) was launched in Tenth Plan for promoting water use efficiency by adopting drip and sprinkler irrigation.

- *Minimum Support Prices (MSP):* Keeping in view the interests of the farmers as also the need of self reliance, Govt. has been announcing minimum support price. The main objectives of announcing MSP are:
  1. To prevent fall in price in the situation of over production.
  2. To protect the interest of farmers by ensuring them a minimum price for their crops in the situation of a price fall in the market.
- *Procurement Prices:* The price at which government buys surplus from the farming coming in the market. The minimum support price and the procurement price may be the same.
- *Issue Prices:* The prices at which fair price shops sell cereals like wheat rice etc.

NEW AGRICULTURAL POLICY (2000)

- Union Government has announced new Agricultural Policy in the parliament on July 28, 2000. This policy has been planned under the provisions of WTO so as to face the challenges of agriculture sector. This policy gives emphasis on promoting agricultural exports after fulfilling domestic demand.
- The sailent features of this policy are:
- To achieve 4% growth rate per annum for the next two decades.
- To do Land reforms to provide land to poor farmers.
- Consolidation of holding in all states of the nation.
- Promoting private investment in agriculture.
- To provide insurance umbrella for crops to farmers.
- To promote biotechnology.

- ❖ Promoting research for developing new varieties and ensuring protection to the developed varieties.
- New Agriculture policy has been described as 'Rainbow Revolution' which includes the following revolutions:

  1. Green   – (Food Grain Production)
  2. White   – (Milk)
  3. Yellow   – (Oil Seeds)
  4. Blue   – (Fisheries)
  5. Red   – (Meat/Tomato)
  6. Golden   – (Fruits-Apple)
  7. Grey   – (Fertiliser)
  8. Black/Brown – (Non-conventional Energy Sources)
  9. Silver   – (Eggs)
  10. Round   – (Potato)

AGRICULTURAL CREDIT

- Agricultural credit is disbursed through a Multi Agency network comprising of Commercial Banks (CBs), Regional Rural Bank (RRBs) and Cooperative with their vast network covering almost all the villages in the country and outreach extending to the remotest part of the country.
- Kisan Credit Card (KCC) scheme was introduced in August, 1998 with major share of crop loans being routed through it. Banks were advised that the credit card should normally be valid for 3 years subject to an annual review.

INDUSTRY

- After independence, the first industrial policy was declared on April 6, 1948 by then Union Industry Minister Mr. Shyama Prasad Mukherjee.
- Under this first industrial policy established a base for Mixed and Controlled Economy in India and clearly divided the industrial sector into private and public sectors.
- Second Industrial Policy Resolution declared on April 30, 1956 with the basic objective of establishing 'Socialistic Pattern of Society' in the country.
- In line with the liberalisation measures announced during the 1980s, the government announced a New Industrial Policy on July 24, 1991. This new policy de-regulates the industrial economy in a substantial manner. The major objectives of the new policy are "to build on the gains already made, correct the distortions or weaknesses that might have crept in, maintain a sustained growth in productivity and gainful employment, and attain international competitiveness."
- During the second five year plan (1956-61) a major task in industry was building up of three steel plants in the public sector—Rourkela Steel Plant in Odisha (then Orissa), Bhilai Steel Plant in Chhattisgarh (then Madhya Pradesh) and Durgapur Steel Plant in West Bengal. The three steel plants came into operation in stage between 1959 and 1962.
- Bokaro steel plant was established in third five year plan.
- In 1973, the Steel Authority of India Limited (SAIL) was created and was made responsible for the development of steel industry.
- Globally, India is the largest producer and second largest exporter of jute goods. There are 78 jute mills in the country of which 61 are in West Bengal, 3 each in Bihar and Uttar Pradesh, 7 in Andhra Pradesh and one each in Assam, Odisha, Tripura and Chhattisgarh.
- Sugar industry occupies an important place among agriculture based industries. This industry took a shape of a large industry in the beginning of 20th century. Sugar industry in the second largest industry after cotton textile industry among agriculture based industries of the country.

General Knowledge

- India is the second largest producer of cement in the world after China. The cement industry was delicensed in 1991.
- The small and medium sector has been defined as micro, small and medium enterprises with effect from October 2, 2006 (the Act defined the medium enterprises for the first time). Further, separate investment limits have been prescribed for manufacturing and service enterprises. The new definition is as follows:

A. Manufacturing Enterprises

(a) A micro enterprise, where the investment in plant and machinery does not exceed ₹ 50 lakh;

(b) A small enterprise, where the investment in plant and machinery is more than ₹ 50 lakh but does not exceed ₹ 10 crore; and

(c) A medium enterprise, where the investment in plant and machinery is more than ₹ 10 crore but does not exceed ₹ 30 crore.

B. Service Enterprises

(a) A micro enterprise, where the investment in equipment does not exceed ₹ 10 lakh;

(b) A small enterprise, where the investment in equipment is more than ₹ 10 lakh but does not exceed ₹ 5 crore; and

(c) A medium enterprise, where the investment in equipment is more than ₹ 5 crore but does not exceed ₹ 15 crore.

- In India, the MSMEs (Micro, Small and Medium Enterprises) play a pivot role in the overall industrial economy of the country. MSMEs contribute about 8 per cent of the GDP of the country, about 45 per cent of manufactured output and about 40 per cent of exports.
- As per the status at the end of December 2017, there are 16 Navratna Companies in India. 8 Companies having Navratna status have been upgraded as 'Maharatna' status holding companies. 'Navratna' status companies are MTNL, Hindustan Petroleum (HPCL), BEL, HAL, Power Finance Corporation (PFC), NMDC. Power Grid Corporation of India Ltd., REC, NALCO, Shipping Corporation of India (SCI), Rashtriya Ispat Nigam Ltd., Oil India Ltd., Niveli Lignite Corporation (NLC), Container Corporation of India Limited, Engineers India Limited and National Buildings Construction Corporation Limited.
- As on end of December 2017 there are 7 'Maharatna' public sector enterprises— SAIL, ONGC, IOC, NTPC, CIL, BHEL, GAIL and BPCL.
- Small Industries Development Bank of India (SIDBI) was set up in 1989. It is a Separate Apex Bank, to provide financial assistance to the small-scale industries.

LABOUR

TRADE UNION

- Trade unions are voluntary organisations of workers formed to protect the interest of workers through collective action.
- In India, the first trade union was formed in 1918.
- There are number of trade unions in India, which are associated with main political parties. Some important trade unions are as follows:
  1. Bharatiya Mazdoor Sangh (BMS), associated with the Bharatiya Janta Party.
  2. Indian National Trade Union Congress (INTUC), associated with the Congress Party.
  3. All-India Trade Union Congress (AITUC), associated with the Communist Party of India.
  4. Centre of Indian Trade Unions (CITU), associated with the CPI (M).

ECONOMIC PLANNING

☞ **Five Year Plans in India**

Plans	Period	Investment (Rs. Crore)	Objectives
First Plan	April 1, 1951-March 31, 1956	1,960	Priority to agriculture, electricity and irrigation.
Second Plan	April 1, 1956—March 31, 1961	4,672	Development of basic and heavy industries.
Third Plan	April 1, 1961—March 31, 1966	8,577	Long term development of India's economy.
Annual Plan	April 1, 1966—March 31, 1967	2,137	
Annual Plan	April 1, 1967—March 31, 1968	2,205	
Annual Plan	April 1, 1968—March 31, 1969	2,283	
Fourth Plan	April 1, 1969—March 31, 1974	15,779	Enlarge the income of rural population and supply of goods of mass consumption.
Fifth Plan	April 1, 1974—March 31, 1979	39,426	Attain increased self-reliance and employment avenues.
Annual Plan	April 1, 1979—March 31, 1980	12,176	
Sixth Plan	April 1, 1980—March 31, 1985	1,09,292	Removal of unemployment
Seventh Plan	April 1, 1985—March 31, 1990	2,18,730	Food work and productivity were the basic priorities.
Eighth Plan	April, 1992—March 31, 1997	4,95,670	Raising employment
Ninth Plan	April 1, 1997—March 31, 2002	9,41,041	Agriculture and rural development
Tenth Plan	April 1, 2002—March 31, 2007	14,91,610	Growth rate 7.8 percent per annum.
Eleventh Plan	April 1, 2007—March 31, 2012	36,44,718	Literacy, Employment, Rural development & Transport development.
Twelfth Plan	April 1, 2012–March 31, 2017	43,30,000	Long term development of India's economy.

12TH FIVE YEAR PLAN

- The salient features of the draft of 12th Plan are—
- ❖ Economic growth target of 8%, meaning India will have to grow at 9% average in last three years of the Plan.
- ❖ Projected investment in infrastructure to grow from 7.10% of GDP in 11th plan to 8.26% of GDP.
- ❖ Total private investment to be 37% of the GDP.
- ❖ Health sector funding to increase by three times.
- ❖ To reduce infant mortality rate, maternal mortality rate and anaemia by 50%.

MONEY AND BANKING

RBI

- Reserve Bank of India (RBI) is the central bank of the country.
- Reserve Bank of India was established on April 1, 1935 under Reserve Bank of India Act, 1934 with a authorised capital of ₹ 5 crore.
- The Reserve Bank of India was nationalised on January 1, 1949.
- The general administration and direction of RBI is managed by a Central Board of Directors consisting of 20 members which includes 1 Governor and 4 Deputy Governors.
- The head office of the Reserve Bank of India is in Mumbai.
- Functions of Reserve Bank of India:
  - ❖ Issue of Notes.
  - ❖ Bankers to the Government.
  - ❖ Banker's Bank.
  - ❖ Controller of Credit.
  - ❖ Custodian of Foreign Reserves.
  - ❖ Other Functions (function of clearing house arranging credit for agriculture, collecting and publishing the economic data, buying and selling of government securities and trade bills etc.)

General Knowledge

Reserve Bank of India	1935
Nationalisation of RBI	1949
State Bank of India	1955
Nationalisation of 14 Commercial Banks	1969
Nationalisation of 6 other Banks	1980
Regional Rural Bank	1975
Merger of New Bank of India with Punjab National Bank	1993
Transformation of IDBI Ltd. as a Scheduled Bank	2004

- **Bank Rate:** Bank Rate is the rate of discount at which the central bank of the country discounts first class bills. It is the rate of interest at which the central bank lends money to the lower banking institutions.

- **Cash Reserve Ratio (CRR):** Commercial banks are required to keep a certain amount of cash reserves at the central bank. This percentage amount is called CRR.

- **Prime Lending Rate (PLR):** Prime Lending Rate (PLR) is that rate of interest at which bank gives loan to its most reliable customer.

- **Repo Rate:** Repo (Repurchase option) rate is a instrument under the Liquidity Adjustment Facility (LAF) at which RBI lends to commercial banks. In case of inflationary tendencies RBI perceived need to inject liquidity into the system, RBI can reduce the Repo rate which will lead to release of money into the market.

- **Reverse Repo Rate:** Reverse Repo Rate is the rate at which RBI borrows from commercial banks. In case of inflationary tendencies, RBI can hike the Reverse Repo rate to absorb the excess liquidity in the market.

- **Statutory Liquidity Ratio (SLR):** Commercial banks are also required to keep (in additon to CRR) a certain percentage of their net demand and time liabilities (NDTL) as liquid assets in the shape of cash, gold or approved securities. As most of the SLR money is kept in treasury bills, government had, in the past, been using SLR as a means to mobilise low cost resources.

☞ **Establishment Years of Major Financial Institutions in India**

❑ Imperial Bank of India	1921
❑ Reserve Bank of India (Nationalisation of RBI took place on January 1, 1949)	April 1, 1935
❑ Industrial Finance Corporation of India (IFCI)	1948
❑ State Bank of India (SBI)	July 1, 1955
❑ Unit Trust of India (UTI)	Feb. 1, 1964
❑ IDBI	July 1964
❑ NABARD	July 12, 1982
❑ IRBI (Now it has been renamed as IIBIL since March 6, 1997)	March 20, 1985
❑ SIDBI	1990
❑ EXIM Bank	January 1, 1982
❑ National Housing Bank (NHB)	July 1988
❑ Life Insurance Corporation (LIC)	September 1956
❑ General Insurance Corporation (GIC)	November 1972
❑ Regional Rural Banks (RRBs)	Oct. 2, 1975
❑ Risk Capital and Technology Finance Corporation Ltd.	March 1975
❑ Technology Development & Information Co. of India Ltd.	1989
❑ Infrastructure Leasing & Financial Services Ltd.	1988
❑ Housing Development Finance Corporation Ltd. (HDFC)	1977

Main Share Price Index in Famous Share Market of the World

BSE (Mumbai)	SENSEX
NSE (Mumbai)	S & P CNX Nifty
New York	DOW JONES
Tokyo	NIKKEI
Frankfurt (Germany)	MID DAX
Hong Kong	HANG SENG
Singapore	SIMEX STRAITS TIMES

PUBLIC FINANCE

- From July 1, 2017 India stepped towards one of the biggest Economic reforms and adopted Goods and Services Tax (GST).
- The Goods and Services Tax (GST) is the most ambitious indirect tax reform plan that seeks to remove severe distortions and flaws in the structure and administration of indirect taxes, both at the Central and the State levels.
- The GST seeks to replace all these Central and State taxes by a single uniform tax both at the Centre and in the States. Thus all local taxes will be subsumed in the GST that will have a uniform rate all across the country. Under the current taxes, only the Centre is empowered to impose service tax. Under the GST regime, the States will also have powers to collect taxes on services.
- Like all other countries, tendency of income tax is progressive in India.
- Estate Duty was first introduced in India in 1953. It was levied on total property passing on the death of a person.
- Service tax was introduced in 1994-95 in a small way to operationalise the principle of neutrality of the tax system to different forms of production and in recognition of the fact that value additions whether in manufacturing or service should form the basis of taxation.
- GST the biggest tax reforms since Independence implemente on July 1, 2017.
- **Revenue Deficit** = Revenue Expenditure – Revenue Receipts
- **Budget Deficit** = Total Expenditure— Total Receipts
- **Fiscal Deficit** = Revenue receipts (Net tax revenue + Non-tax revenue) + Capital receipts (only recoveries of loans and other receipts)– Total expenditure (Plan and non-plan)
- **Primary Deficit:** The excess of fiscal deficit over payments of interest is called primary deficit.

☞ **Important Committees: At a Glance**

Committies	Related Area
Hanumant Rao Committee	*Fertilisers*
Mahajan Committee	*Sugar Industry*
R.V. Gupta Committee	*Agriculture Credit*
Narsimham Committee (Second)	*Banking Reforms*
CB Bhave Committee	*Company Information*
S.L. Kapoor Committee	*Credit & Flow Problems of SSIs*
Mashelkar Committee	*Auto Fuel Policy*
Bhurelal Committee	*Increase in Motor Vehicle Tax*
Abhijit Sen Committee	*Long Term Food Policy*
Kelkar Committee	*Tax Structure Reforms*
J.J. Irani Committee	*Company Law Reforms*
Parekh Committee	*Infrastructure Financing*

General Knowledge

General
SCIENCE

PHYSICS

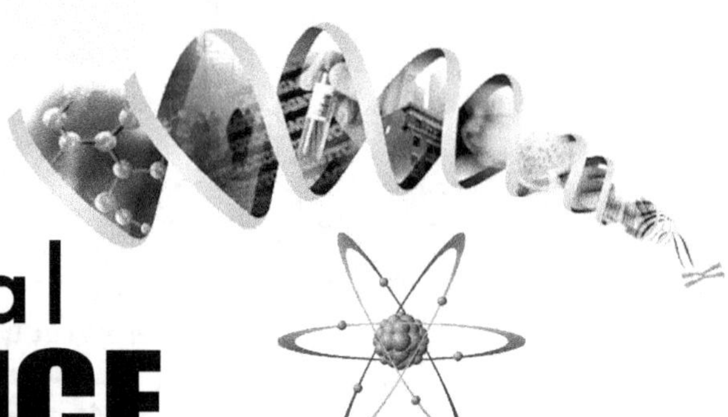

PHYSICAL QUANTITIES

- Physical quantities may be divided in two classes:
  1. Scalar Quantities
  2. Vector Quantities
- A scalar quantity is one which has only magnitude.
- A vector quantity has both magnitude and direction.
- Force, Velocity, Momentum, Acceleration are examples of vector quantities.
- Mass, length, time, volume, speed, energy, work are examples of scalar quantities.

UNITS

- All measurements in physics require standard units.
- In 1960, the General Conference of Weights and Measures recommended that a metric system of measurements called the International System of Units, abbreviated as SI units, be used.

☞ **Some Important Units**

S.No.	Units	Quantity
1.	Metre	Length
2.	Kilogram	Mass
3.	Second	Time
4.	Ampere	Electric Current
5.	Candela	Luminous Intensity
6.	Newton	Force
7.	Joule	Workdone
8.	Watt	Power
9.	Coulomb	Quantity of Electricity
10.	Volt	Potential Difference
11.	Ohm	Electrical Resistance
12.	Farad	Capacitance
13.	Henry	Inductance
14.	Lumen	Luminous Flux

- Very small distances are measured in micro-meters or (microns) (μm), angstroms ($\overset{\circ}{A}$), nanometers (nm) and femtometres (fm).

MOTION

- When a body changes its position with respect to something else as time goes on, we say the body is in motion.
- There are two types of motion—translational (linear) and rotational (spin).
- The motion of a car on a road is translational whereas the motion of a top, spinning on its axis is rotational.

SPEED

- It is a scalar form of velocity and is defined as the distance travelled in one second.

- Speed = $\dfrac{\text{distance travelled}}{\text{time required}}$
- SI unit of speed is m/s.

VELOCITY

- The distance covered by an object in a specified direction in unit time interval is called velocity.
- The SI unit of velocity is m/s.
- Velocity is a vector quantity.

ACCELERATION

- The velocity of a body changes due to change in its speed or direction or both. The rate of change of the velocity of a body is called its acceleration.
- Acceleration = $\dfrac{\text{change in velocity}}{\text{time}}$

FORCE AND MOTION

GRAVITATIONAL FORCE

- It is the force of attraction between two masses.
- It is gravitational force that holds the moon in its orbit round the earth and the earth in its orbit round the sun.
- *Newton's Law of Universal Gravitation* states that every particle in the universe attracts every other particle with a force that is directly proportional to the product of their masses and inversely proportional to the square of the distance between them.
- The value of G is 6.67×10^{-11} SI units.

CENTRIPETAL FORCE

- The force acting towards the centre on a particle executing uniform circular motion is called centripetal force and is given by

$$F = \dfrac{mv^2}{r}$$

where, m = Mass of the object

v = Speed

r = Radius of the Circular Path

- In case of the moon, gravitational force between the earth and the moon acts as the centripetal force.
- Centripetal force always acts on the particle performing circular motion.

CENTRIFUGAL FORCE

- The pseudo force that balances the centripetal force in uniform circular motion is called centrifugal force.
- Centrifugal force is directed away from the centre along the radius.
- The centrifugal force is zero exactly at the poles and maximum at the equator.

WEIGHT

- The weight of a body is the force with which the earth attracts the body towards its centre.
- The mass of a body is a constant quantity whereas its weight varies slightly from place-to-place on the earth.
- The weight of a body is maximum at the poles and minimum at the equator. This variation in weight is due to:
1. the shape of the earth.
2. the rotation of the earth about its axis.
- The weight of an object is less at high elevations than at sea level.
- At the centre of the earth, the weight of a body would be zero.
- On the surface of the moon the value of the acceleration due to gravity is nearly one-sixth of that on earth and, therefore, an object on the moon would weigh only one-sixth its weight on the earth. The mass of an object on the moon would be the same as on earth.
- The weight of a body would be more if the earth stopped rotating. Conversely, if the speed of rotation were higher, the weight would be less.
- A person weighs more in a lift, which is accelerating upward.
- An astronaut feels weightless in a spaceship because he is not pushing against anything.

General Knowledge

FRICTION

- Friction is the force which opposes the relative motion of two surfaces in contact.
- It is friction between the ground and the soles of our shoes that makes walking possible and it is lack of friction that makes our feet slip on highly polished surfaces.
- Friction in machines wastes energy and also causes wear and tear. This friction is reduced by using (1) lubricants, and (2) ball bearings.

NEWTON'S LAWS OF MOTION

First Law

- Every object continues in its state of rest or of uniform motion in a straight line if no net force acts upon it. It is also known as *law of inertia*.
- **Examples:** 1. An unwary passenger in a fast-moving bus falls forward when it stops suddenly. This happens because the feet of the passenger come to rest suddenly whereas his body continues to be in motion. 2. A person getting down from a moving bus has to run some distance, in the direction of the bus, before stopping. If he does not run he is bound to fall because his feet come to rest whereas his body continues to be in motion.

Momentum

- The momentum of a body is defined as the product of its mass and velocity.

Second Law

- This law states that "the rate of change of momentum of a body is proportional to the applied force and takes place in the direction of the force."
- If we express force (F) in Newtons, mass (m) in kilograms and acceleration (a) in metres per second squared, we can write the second law as; $F = ma$.
- In travelling the same distance, a car consumes more fuel on a crowded road than on a free road. This happens because the car has to stop and start quite often on a crowded road. The repeated acceleration requires a force (second law), which ultimately comes from the fuel. On a free road the car runs at almost uniform speed requiring fewer accelerations and hence less fuel consumption.

Third Law

- This law states that "to every action there is an equal and opposite reaction."
- When a bullet is fired from a gun, equal and opposite forces are exerted on the bullet and the gun.
- The engine in a jet aeroplane works on the same principle as a rocket but there is a difference in the method of obtaining the high velocity as jet.

IMPULSE

- If a force acts on a body for a very short time, then the product of force and time is called the impulse.

  Impulse = Change in momentum

  = Force × Time

Application of Impulse

1. A cricket player draws his hand back while catching.
2. A person jumping on hard cement floor receives more injuries than a person jumping on muddy or sandy floor.

WORK, POWER AND ENERGY

WORK

- Whenever a force acting on a body displaces it, work is said to be done. Work = Force × Distance moved in the direction of force.
- Work is a scalar quantity and its SI unit is Joule (J).

POWER

- Power is defined as the rate of doing work.

$$Power = \frac{Work\ done}{Time\ taken}$$

- The SI unit of power is Watt (W) and is also measured in horse power.

  1 HP = 746 W

 **General Knowledge**

ENERGY

- Energy is defined as the capacity to do work.

Kinetic Energy

- The energy possessed by an object due to its motion is called kinetic energy and is described by the expression

$$KE = \frac{1}{2}mv^2$$; where, m = mass of the object

$$v = \text{speed}$$

☞ **Transformation of Energy**

S.No.	Equipment	Transformation
1.	Dynamo	Mechanical energy into electrical energy
2.	Microphone	Sound energy into electrical energy
3.	Loud Speaker	Electrical energy into sound energy
4.	Electric Bulb	Electrical energy into light and heat energy
5.	Battery	Chemical energy into electrical energy
6.	Electrical Motor	Electrical energy into mechanical energy

CENTRE OF GRAVITY

- The centre of gravity of a body is the point where the whole weight of the body can be considered to act.

- Racing cars are build low and with wide wheel bases to reduce the risk of overturning at sharp bends.

- While crossing a river in a boat, passengers are not allowed to stand. This keeps the CG of the system (boat and passengers) low and ensures stability.

ARTIFICIAL SATELLITES

- In the case of a satellite, the centripetal force is provided by the gravitational pull of the earth.

- If the speed of a satellite is more than 11.2 km/s or 25,000 miles/hour, the satellite would escape the earth entirely and would never come back. This is called escape velocity.

- The existence of gaseous atmosphere on the earth is due to the high value of its escape velocity.

Geostationary Satellites

- Geostationary satellites are stationary with respect to an observer on the earth. Their time period is 24-hour. There height above the surface of earth is 36,000 km. They are always in equatorial plane and their orbits are circular. They are also called parking orbits.

DENSITY AND RELATIVE DENSITY

DENSITY

- The mass per unit volume of a substance is called its density.

$$\text{Density} = \frac{\text{Mass}}{\text{Volume}}$$

- The SI unit of density is kilogram per metre cubed (kg/m^3).

- The relative density of a substance is the ratio of the density of the substance to the density of water.

- Relative density has no unit.

PRESSURE

- Pressure is defined as force acting per unit area.

$$\text{Pressure} = \frac{\text{Force}}{\text{Area}}$$

Potential Energy

- Potential energy is the energy possessed by the body by virtue of its position, configuration or any condition of stress or strain.

- There are many examples of potential energy. A stone held at some height above the ground has potential energy. Water in an elevated reservoir possesses potential energy.

General Knowledge

- The SI unit of pressure is newton per metre squared or pascal.
- Broad wooden sleepers are placed below the rails to reduce the pressure exerted by the weight of a train.
- The pressure of water increases with depth, therefore bottom of a dam is made much thicken than the top.
- The pressure exerted on an enclosed liquid at one place is transmitted equally throughout the liquid. This is called Pascal's Principle.
- Hydraulic presses, hydraulic brakes, hydraulic door closers, etc. are applications of the Pascal's Principle.
- At high attitudes where atmosphere pressure is less nose bleeding may occur due to the greater pressure of blood.
- In an aircraft flying at high altitude, normal atmospheric pressure is maintained by the use of air pumps. If this were not done, the crew and passengers would experience difficulty in breathing and consequently face dangers.
- Atmospheric pressure is measured with an instrument called the *Barometer*.

ARCHIMEDE'S PRINCIPLE

- This principle states that when a body is wholly or partially immersed in a fluid, it experiences an upthrust (upward force) equal to the weight of the fluid displaced.
- An iron nail sinks in water whereas a ship made of iron and steel floats. This is due to the fact that a ship is hollow and contains air and, therefore, its density is less than that of water.
- The density of sea water is more than that of river water, due to this a ship sinks less in sea water. It is for this reason that a ship rises a little when it enters a sea from a river.
- It is because of the higher density of sea water that it is easier to swim in the sea.
- A balloon filled with a light gas, such as hydrogen, rises because the average density of the balloon and the gas is less than that of air. The balloon cannot rise indefinitely because the density of the air decreases with increasing altitude. At a certain height, where the density of air is equal to the average density of the balloon, it ceases to rise and drifts sideways with the wind.
- When an ice block floats in water the water level will remain the same when all the ice melts into water.
- A *hydrometer* is an instrument used for measuring the relative density of liquids.
- A special type of a hydrometer called *Lactometer* is used for testing milk by measuring its density.

SURFACE TENSION

- Surface tension is that property of liquids owing to which they tend to acquire minimum surface area.
- Surface tension is caused by molecular attractions.
- When a paint brush is dipped in water all its hair spread out but when it is taken out it is covered with a thin film of water which contracts due to surface tension and pulls the hair together.
- Liquid drops, such as raindrops, oildrops, drops of molten metals, dewdrops etc. are all spherical because their surface tend to contract in order to have minimum surface area. For a given volume, a sphere has the minimum surface area.
- Soaps and detergents lower the surface tension of water. This increases the wetting power of water or its ability to detach dirt particles from clothes and untensils.
- The force of attraction between unlike molecules is called **adhesion** and that between like molecules **cohesion.**
- The melted wax of a candle is drawn up

into the wick by capillary action. Oil rises up a lamp wick for the same reason.

- If one end of a sugar cube is dipped into tea, the entire cube is quickly wet on account of capillary action.

VISCOSITY

- The force which opposes the relative motion between different layers of liquid or gases is called viscous force.
- Viscosity is the property of liquids and gases both.

BERNOULLI'S THEOREM

- According to Bernoulli's theorem, in case of streamline flow of incompressible and non-viscous fluid (ideal fluid) through a tube, total energy (sum of pressure energy, potential energy and kinetic energy) per unit volume of fluid is same at all points.
1. When a bowler spins a ball, it changes its direction (swings) in the air due to unequal pressure acting on it.

HEAT

- Heat is that form of energy which flows from one body to other body due to difference in temperature between the bodies. The amount of heat contained in a body depends upon the mass of the body.

TEMPERATURE

- The temperature of a body is the quantity that tells how hot or cold it is with respect to some standard body.

MEASUREMENT OF TEMPERATURE

- Temperature is measured by a thermometer.
- A thermometer may be graduated in following scales—
1. The upper and lower points of centigrade scale are 100°C and 0°C.
2. The upper and lower points of Fahrenheit scale are 212°F and 32°F.
3. The upper and lower points of Reaumur scale are 80°R and 0°R.
4. The upper and lower points of Kelvin scale are 373K and 273K.
5. The upper and lower points of Rankine scale are 672° Ra and 460° Ra.

- At −40 degrees both celsius and Fahrenheit scales will show identical readings.
- Water cannot be used in a thermometer becaues it freezes at 0°C and also because of its irregular expansion.

THERMAL EXPANSION

- Solids, liquids and gases generally expand when heated and contract when cooled.
- Gaps have to be left in railway tracks to make allowance for expansion, otherwise the rails will buckle. Allowance is made for the expansion of long steel bridges. One end of such bridge is fixed while the other rests on rollers.
- Telephone wires sag more in summer than in winter due to thermal expansion.

EXPANSION OF WATER

- Water has its minimum volume and maximum density at 4°C.

TRANSMISSION OF HEAT

- There are three ways of heat transmission: 1. Conduction; 2. Convection; 3. Radiation.

Conduction

- In this process, heat is transferred from one place to other place by the successive vibration of the particles of the medium without bodily movement of the particles of the medium.
- Conduction takes place mainly in solids.
- Air is a very bad conductor of heat. The good insulating properties of wool, cotton, etc. are mainly due to the air spaces they contain.

General Knowledge

Convection

- In this process, heat is transferred by the actual movement of particles of the medium from one place to other place.
- In liquids and gases heat is transmitted by convection.

Radiation

- In this mode of heat transmission heat is transferred from one place to another without effecting the intervening medium.

HEAT CAPACITY

- The heat capacity of a body is defined as the heat required to raise the temperature of the body by 1K. Its SI unit is J/K.

SPECIFIC HEAT CAPACITY

- The specific heat capacity of a substance is the heat required to raise the temperature of a unit mass of the substance by 1K.
- Its SI unit is J/kg K.
- It is because of its high specific heat capacity that water is used as a cooling liquid in car engine.

LATENT HEAT

- It is defined as the amount of heat absorbed or given out by a body during the change of state.
- Each gram of ice that melts absorbs 336 J of heat.

EVAPORATION

- Water can change into the vapour state either by boiling or by evaporation at lower temperatures.
- When sweat evaporates from the skin it draws much heat from the body and produces a cooling sensation.
- In summer, water is stored in pitchers for cooling. Water oozes out of the pores of the pitchers and cools on evaporation.
- The rate of evaporation increases with increase in temperature.

REFRIGERATOR

- In a refrigerator, cooling is produced by the evaporation of a volatile liquid, freon, inside a copper coil (evaporator), which surrounds the freezer.
- The cooling unit (freezer) in a refrigerator is fitted near the top to cool the whole of the interior.

RELATIVE HUMIDITY

- Relative humidity is defined as the ratio of the mass of water vapour in a given volume of air to the mass required for saturating the same volume of air at the same temperature.
- Relative humidity is measured with an instrument called the hygrometer.

PRESSURE COOKER

- The boiling point of a liquid depends on external pressure.
- When the atmospheric pressure is 76 cm of mercury, water boils at 100°C. But when the pressure is increased, the boiling point of water is raised.
- In a pressure cooker, water boils at temperatures higher than 100°C due to increased pressure. The increased boiling temperature allows water to hold more heat which cooks food faster.
- At higher altitudes, atmospheric pressure is reduced. This lowers the boiling point of water and food takes much longer to cook.

WAVE MOTION

- Wave motion may be defined as the transfer of energy without the net transfer of matter.
- If the particles of the medium vibrate perpendicular to the direction of propagation of wave, the wave is called transverse wave.
- Light waves are transverse waves.

- If the particles of the medium vibrate in the direction of propagation of wave, the wave is called longitudinal wave.
- Sound waves are longitudinal waves.

ELECTROMAGNETIC WAVE

- Electromagnetic waves include an enormous range of frequencies—from radio waves with frequencies less than 10^5 Hz to gamma rays having frequencies greater than 10^{20} Hz.
- All electromagnetic wave have the same speed (3×10^8 m/s) in vacuum. The relation $V = n\lambda$ holds good for all electromagnetic waves.

RADIO AND TELEVISION TRANSMISSION

- Radio waves sent out by radio stations are reflected by the ionosphere and can be received anywhere on the earth.
- At night the radio reception improves because the layers of the ionosphere are not exposed to sunlight and are more settled.
- Radar (Radio detection and ranging) employs high frequency radio waves for detecting objects like ships and aeroplanes.
- In microwave oven, when the waves fall on the food, these are absorbed by water, fats, sugars and certain other molecules whose consequent vibrations produce heat. Since heating occurs inside the food, without warming the surrounding air, the cooking time is greatly reduced.
- In microwave oven, food cannot be cooked in metal vessels because the metal blocks out the microwaves.

LIGHT

- Light is a form of energy which is propagated as electromagnetic waves.
- Light is a transverse wave.
- Speed of light in vacuum is 3×10^8 m/s.
- Light takes 8 minute 16.6 second to reach from sun to earth.

REFLECTION

- When light is incident upon a surface, part of it is reflected. But certain surfaces like mirrors and polished metals reflect almost all the light incident upon them.
- The law of reflection states that the angle of incidence is equal to the angle of reflection.
- To see his full image in a plane mirror, a person requires a mirror of at least half of his height.

INCLINED MIRROR (No. of Images)

- When an object is placed between two inclined mirrors, several images of the object are formed.

CURVED MIRRORS

- There are two types of curved spherical mirrors—1. Concave Mirror, 2. Convex Mirror.
- Concave mirror can concentrate the sun's radiation falling on it at one point, it can be used as a burning glass.
- Concave mirrors are also used in solar cookers.
- Large concave mirrors are used in reflecting telescopes for observing and photographing distant stars and other heavenly bodies.
- Concave mirror is also used as a shaving or make-up mirror.
- Small concave mirrors are used by dentists for examining teeth.
- Concave parabolic mirrors are used in searchlight and headlamps of cars.
- Convex mirrors are also used as rear view mirrors in vehicles.

REFRACTION

- When a ray of light passes from one medium to other it suffers a change in direction at the boundary of separation of two media. This phenomenon is called refraction.

General Knowledge

- When a ray passes from one medium to another optically denser medium, e.g., from air to water or glass, it bends towards the normal. Conversely, a ray passing from water or glass into air is bent away from the normal.
- Rivers appear shallow, coin in a beaker filled with water appears raised, due to refraction.
- Another effect of refraction is the apparent upward bending of the immersed portion of a stick when dipped in water.
- It is due to refraction, produced by the earth's atmosphere, that the sun is visible for several minutes after it has set below the horizon. Thus, atmospheric refraction tends to lengthen the day.
- When the sun (or moon) is near the horizon, it appears elliptical, i.e., with the vertical diameter less than the horizontal diameter. This happens because rays from the lower edge of the sun are bent more then those from the upper edge (Atmospheric Refraction).
- One of the most interesting effects of atmospheric refraction and Mirage is a combined effect of atmospheric refraction and total internal reflection.

DISPERSION

- White light consists of seven colours— violet, indigo, blue, green, yellow, orange and red. These colours are called the spectrum of the white light.
- Violet has the minimum wavelength (or maximum frequency) and red the maximum wavelength (or minimum frequency).
- Due to different speeds, the colours are refracted through different angles and therefore, when a narrow beam of white light passes through a glass prism, it is split up into its constituent colours. This separation of light into colours is called dispersion.

COLOUR OF OBJECTS

- We see objects because of the light they reflect.
- When a rose is viewed in white light, its petals appear red and the leaves appear green, because the petals reflect the red part of the white light and leaves reflect the green part. The remaining colours are absorbed. When the same rose is viewed in green light, the petals will appear black and the leaves green. In blue or yellow light both the petals and leaves will appear black.
- Red, blue and green and primary colours.

LENSES

- There are mainly two types of lenses:
  1. Convex or Converging Lens
  2. Concave or Diverging Lens
- Converging or convex lens is used as a magnifying glass.
- Power of a lens is its capacity to deviate a ray. Power of a lens is measured as the reciprocal of the focal length.

$$P = \frac{1}{f}$$

- SI unit of power of lens is dioptre (D).
- The power of a converging lens is positive and that of a diverging lens is negative.
- For all positions of the object, the images formed by diverging (concave) lens are virtual, erect and diminished.

EYE

- The light entering the eye is focused by the eye-lens to form an image on the retina.
- In front of the eye lens is the coloured part of eye, called the iris, which auto-matically adjusts the size of the pupil to the intensity of light falling on it.
- In bright light the iris automatically shuts tighter, reducing the amount of

light entering the pupil. This protects the retina from getting damaged.

- When a person enters a dark room after being in bright light, he is not able to see clearly for a while because the iris is unable to dilate the pupil immediately.
- Least distance of distinct vision is 25 cm.

DEFECTS OF VISION

- A person suffering from long sight (hyper-metropia) can clearly see objects at infinity but cannot see near objects clearly. This defect is caused by the eyeball being too short and can be corrected by wearing converging lenses.
- In the case of a person suffering from short sight (myopia), the eye ball is too long and distant objects are focused in front of the retina. This defect can be corrected by wearing diverging lenses.
- *Astigmatism:* Curvature of cornea becomes irregular and image is not clear. Cylindrical lens is used.

SCATTERING OF LIGHT

- When light falls on atoms and molecules, it is scattered in all directions.
- Scattering of light is maximum for violet colour and minimum for red colour.
- Blue colour of sky is due to scattering of light.
- In the evening, the sun is lower in the sky and its light has to traverse a longer path through the atmosphere to reach an observer. Thus, at sunset, blue, green and other colours having been scattered only red and some orange light reach us and the sun appears a deep orange-red.
- In outerspace, i.e., beyond the atmosphere, there is nothing to scatter the sunlight and therefore the sky appears dark and stars are visible even in the presence of the sun.

INTERFERENCE OF LIGHT

- The superposition of two (or more) waves of the same kind that pass the same point in space at the same time is called interference.
- Beautiful colours seen in soap bubbles and oil films on water are produced due to the interference of white light reflected by these surfaces.
- LASER (Light Amplification by Stimulated Emission of Radiation) is an optical device which produces an intense beam of coherent monochromatic light.
- Examples of Interference of Light: Holography, Laser.

DIFFRACTION OF LIGHT

- When a beam of light passes through a narrow slit or an aperture, it spreads out to a certain extent into the region of geometrical shadow. This is an example of diffraction, i.e., of the failure of light to travel in a straight line.

SOUND

- Sound waves are longitudinal and cannot travel in vacuum. The transmission of sound requires a medium: air, liquid or solid.
- The longitudinal mechanical waves which lie in the frequency range 20 Hz to 20,000 Hz are called audible or sound waves. These waves are sensitive to human ear.
- The longitudinal mechanical waves having frequencies less than 20 Hz are called Infrasonic. These waves are produced by sources of bigger size such as earthquakes, volcanic eruptions, ocean waves etc.
- The longitudinal waves having frequencies greater than 20,000 Hz are called ultrasonic waves. Human ear cannot detect these waves. But some animals such as cats, dogs, bats can detect these waves.

PITCH

- The pitch (shrillness of a sound depends on its frequency.

General Knowledge 

- A sound of higher frequency has a higher pitch.
- The pitch of a woman's voice is higher than that of a man.

LOUDNESS

- The relative loudness of a sound is measured in decibels (db).
- All stringed instruments, such as the violin, sitar, guitar, etc. have sound boxes attached to increase the loudness.

SPEED OF SOUND

- The presence of water vapour in the air increases the speed of sound.
- Sound travels faster through warm air than through cold air. The speed of sound is higher on a hot day than on a cold day.
- Thunder is heard much after the flash of lighting is seen because of the wide difference in the speeds of light and sound.

REFLECTION OF SOUND

- When a sound wave is reflected by a distant obstacle, such as a wall or a cliff, an echo is heard.
- To hear echo, the minimum distance between the observer and reflector should be 17 m.
- Exploration of underwater gas and oil is done by detecting the echoes of shock waves produced by explosions on the water surface.
- Bats emit ultrasonic waves of frequencies up to 80,000 Hz and use the reflection of these waves (echoes) to determine the presence and distance of objects on their way and from them respectively.

DOPPLER EFFECT

- The Doppler effect is the change in frequency of a wave (sound or light) due to the motion of the source or observer.
- It is due to the Doppler effect that the whistle of a train appears shriller when it approaches a listener than when it moves away from him.

ELECTRICITY

- Electricity produced by friction between two dissimilar objects is known as static electricity. Depending on the nature of the objects, one acquires a positive charge and the other an equal negative charge. For example, if a glass rod is rubbed with silk, the rod acquires positive charge and the silk an equal negative charge.
- *Lightning* is a gigantic electric discharge occurring between two charged clouds or between a charged cloud and the earth.

CONDUCTOR

- Conductors are those materials which allow electricity (charge) to pass through themselves.
- Metals conduct electricity because they have a large number of conduction or free electrons.

INSULATORS

- Insulators are those materials which do not allow electricity to flow through themselves. Insulators have no free electrons.

SUPER CONDUCTORS

- The resistance of metals to flow of electricity reduces with decreasing temperature. At temperatures near absolute zero, metals have almost zero resistance and became super conductors.

SEMI-CONDUCTORS

- Certain materials, such as silicon and germanium, have electrical resistivity intermediate between those of conductors and insulators. These materials are termed as semi-conductors.

General Knowledge

- Semi-conductors are good insulators in their pure crystalline form but their conductivity increases when small amounts of impurities are added to them.

ELECTRIC CURRENT

- Electric current is simply the flow of electric charge. In solid conductors the flow of electrons and in fluids the flow of ions as well as electrons constitute the current.
- SI units of electric current is Ampere (A).

ELECTRICAL RESISTANCE

- When electric current flows through a conductor, e.g., a metallic wire, it offers some obstruction to the current. This obstruction offered by the wire is called its electrical resistance.
- SI unit of Resistance is ohm.

OHM'S LAW

- If physical conditions like temperature, intensity of light etc. remains unchanged then electric current flowing through a conductor is directly proportional to the potential difference across its ends.

ELECTRIC MOTOR

- In an electric motor, electrical energy is converted into mechanical energy.
- Electric fans, mixers, washing machines, etc. work on electric motors.

INVERTER

- An inverter is a device which converts DC to AC. The inverters used in homes and offices are specially designed to:
  1. Convert DC from a battery to AC, and
  2. Charge the battery.

FUSE

- Electric fuse is a protective device used in series with an electric appliance to save it from being damaged due to high current.
- A fuse is a short piece of wire made of a tin-lead alloy, which has a low melting point.

- Fuses are always connected in the live wire.

COST OF ELECTRICITY

- The consumption of electrical energy in a house is measured in the unit kWh.
- Kilowatt hour is equal to the energy consumed in the circuit at the rate of 1 kilowatt for 1 hour.

MAGNETISM

- A magnet attracts and holds pieces of iron but does not attract pieces of copper.
- Iron, cobalt, nickel and certain alloys are strongly magnetic whereas copper, wood, glass, etc. are non-magnetic.
- Our earth behaves as a powerful magnet whose south pole is near the geographical north pole and whose north pole is near the geographical south pole.

ATOMIC & NUCLEAR PHYSICS

- Atom consists of three fundamental particles electron, proton and neutron. All the protons and neutrons are present in the central core of atom called nucleus. Electrons revolve around the nucleus.
- The total number of protons in the nucleus is called atomic number (Z).
- The total number of proton and neutrons in the nucleus is called mass number (A).
- Ernest Rutherford, discovered nucleus by the scattering of α-particles from gold foil.

RADIOACTIVITY

- Henry Bacquerel (1896) observed that a photographic plate blackened, when placed near double sulphate of potassium and uranium. He further observed that uranium emitted special kind of rays. They were called Becqueral rays.

General Knowledge

- Pierre and Marie Curie observed that the radiation from pitchblende was four times stronger than uranium. In 1898, they finally discovered two new substances—Polonium and Radium. These newly discovered substances were called radioactive substances and this property of these substances was named radioactivity.

- No radioactive substance emits both α and β particles simultaneously.

X-RAYS

- X-rays are electromagnetic radiations having wavelength from a fraction of an Angestrom to about 100Å. They were discovered by Rontgen during his studies on the electrical discharge phenomena in gases—he found that an unknown radiation was produced when electrons collided with the walls of the tubes.

ATOMIC ENERGY

- India today ranks sixth in the atomic energy programmes. It has developed the required know-how and expertise to manufacture nuclear weapons, but it believes in the peaceful uses of atomic power. The Atomic Energy Commission was set-up in the country in 1948 under the Chairmanship of Dr. H. J. Bhabha.

- ***Bhabha Atomic Research Centre (BARC):*** The Bhabha Atomic Research Centre at Trombay near Mumbai (Maharashtra) has four research reactors: (*i*) APSARA—It is the first atomic reactor in Asia; (*ii*) CIRUS—It is a joint Indo-Canadian project; (*iii*) PURNIMA II—a zero energy fast reactor, and (*iv*) DHRUVA—a high power completely indigenous nuclear research reactor with most advanced laboratories in the world. Another fast breeder reactor KAMINI at Kalpakkam has been constructed. Today India is the seventh country in the world and the first developing nation to have mastered the fast breeder reactor technology.

- **Nuclear Power:** Under Nuclear Power Corporation of India Limited (NPCIL) there are seven nuclear power stations in operation in six States: (*i*) Tarapur—Maharashtra, (*ii*) Rawatbhata—Rajasthan, (*iii*) Kalpakkam—Tamil Nadu, (*iv*) Narora—U.P., (*v*) Kakrapara—Gujarat, (*vi*) Kaiga—Karnataka and (*vii*) Kudankulam—Tamil Nadu. Six more reactors of 4300 MWE unit size are under construction at Kalpakkam, Kakrapara, Rawatbhata and Kudankulam.

- **Heavy Water:** Heavy water is one of the essential input for Pressurised Heavy Water Reactors (PHWRs) used both as a coolant and moderator. The first heavy water plant was set-up in 1962 in Nangal. Subsequently 7 more plants have been set-up at (*i*) Baroda, (*ii*) Tuticorin, (*iii*) Kota, (*iv*) Talcher, (*v*) Thal, (*vi*) Hazira and (*vii*) Manuguru.

- **Research and Development Centres:** Four research centres namely (*i*) Bhabha Atomic Research Centre, Trombay (Maharashtra), (*ii*) Indira Gandhi Centre for Atomic Research, Kalpakkam (Tamil Nadu), (*iii*) Centre for Advanced Technology, Indore (Madhya Pradesh), (*iv*) Variable Energy Cyclotron Centre at Kolkata (West Bengal) are focal points of research and development work in nuclear energy and related discipline.

- **India's Nuclear Explosions:** On May 18, 1974 India conducted her first underground nuclear explosion at Pokhran (Rajasthan) in the Thar desert, 20 km. away from Jaisalmer, at a depth of more than 100 metres. The successful explosion made India the sixth nuclear nation in the world.

- India conducted 5 nuclear explosion tests at Pokhran in two phases on May 11 and May 13, 1998 and became a nuclear power state.

Name of Invention	Inventor	Nationality	Year
Aeroplane	Orville & Wilbur Wright	U.S.A.	1903
Ball-Point Pen	John J. Loud	U.S.A.	1888
Barometer	Evangelista Torricelli	Italy	1644
Bicycle	Kirkpatrick Macmillan	Britain	1839-40
Bifocal Lens	Benjamin Franklin	U.S.A.	1780
Car (Petrol)	Karl Benz	Germany	1888
Celluloid	Alexander Parkes	Britain	1861
Cinema	Nicolas & Jean Lumiere	France	1895
Clock (mechanical)	I-Hsing & Liang Ling-Tsan	China	725
Diesel Engine	Rudolf Diesel	Germany	1895
Dynamo	Hypolite Pixii	France	1832
Electric Lamp	Thomas Alva Edison	U.S.A.	1879
Electric Motor (DC)	Zenobe Gramme	Belgium	1873
Electric Motor (AC)	Nikola Tesla	U.S.A.	1888
Electro-magnet	William Sturgeon	Britain	1824
Electronic Computer	Dr. Alan M. Turing	Britain	1943
Film (moving outlines)	Louis Prince	France	1885
Film (musical sound)	Dr. Le de Forest	U.S.A.	1923
Fountain Pen	Lewis E. Waterman	U.S.A.	1884
Gramophone	Thomas Alva Edison	U.S.A.	1878
Helicopter	Etienne Oehmichen	France	1924
Jet Engine	Sir Frank Whittle	Britain	1937
Laser	Charles H. Townes	U.S.A.	1960
Lift (Mechanical)	Elisha G. Otis	U.S.A.	1852
Locomotive	Richard Trevithick	Britain	1804
Machine Gun	James Puckle	Britain	1718
Microphone	Alexander Graham Bell	U.S.A.	1876
Microscope	Z. Janssen	Netherlands	1590
Motor Cycle	G. Daimler	Germany	1885
Photography (on film)	John Carbutt	U.S.A.	1888
Printing Press	Johann Gutenberg	Germany	c.1455
Razor (safety)	King C. Gillette	U.S.A.	1895
Refrigerator	James Harrison & Alexander Catlin	U.S.A.	1850
Safety Pin	Walter Hunt	U.S.A.	1849
Sewing machine	Barthelemy Thimmonnier	France	1829
Ship (steam)	J.C. Perier	France	1775
Ship (turbine)	Hon. Sir C. Parsons	Britain	1894
Skyscraper	W. Le Baron Jenny	U.S.A.	1882
Slide Rule	William Oughtred	Britain	1621
Steam Engine (condenser)	James Watt	Britain	1765
Steel Production	Henry Bessemer	Britain	1855
Steel (stainless)	Harry Brearley	Britain	1913
Submarine	David Bushnell	U.S.A.	1776
Tank	Sir Ernest Swinton	Britain	1914
Telegraph	M. Lammond	France	1787
Telegraph Code	Samuel F.B. Morse	U.S.A.	1837

General Knowledge

Name of Invention	Inventor	Nationality	Year
Telephone (perfected)	Alexander Graham Bell	U.S.A.	1876
Television (mechanical)	John Logie Baird	Britain	1926
Television (electronic)	P.T. Farnsworth	U.S.A.	1927
Thermometer	Galileo Galilei	Italy	1593
Transformer	Michael Faraday	Britain	1831
Transistor	Bardeen, Shockley & Brattain	U.S.A.	1948
Washing Machine (elec.)	Hurley Machine Co.	U.S.A.	1907
Zip-Fastener	W.L. Judson	U.S.A.	1891

☞ IMPORTANT DISCOVERIES

Discovery	Discoverer	Nationality	Year
Aluminium	Hans Christian Oerstedt	Denmark	1827
Atomic number	Henry Moseley	England	1913
Atomic structure of matter	John Dalton	England	1803
Chlorine	C.W. Scheele	Sweden	1774
Electromagnetic induction	Michael Faraday	England	1831
Electromagnetic waves	Heinrich Hertz	Germany	1886
Electromagnetism	Hans Christian Oersted	Denmark	1920
Electron	Sir Joseph Thomson	England	1897
General theory of relativity	Albert Einstein	Switzerland	1915
Hydrogen	Henry Cavendish	England	1766
Law of electric conduction	Georg Ohm	Germany	1827
Law of electromagnetism	Andre Ampere	France	1826
Law of falling bodies	Galileo	Italy	1590
Laws of gravitation & motion	Isaac Newton	England	1687
Laws of planetary motion	Johannes Kepler	Germany	1609-10
Magnesium	Sir Humphry Davy	England	1808
Neptune (Planet)	Johann Galle	Germany	1846
Neutron	James Chadwick	England	1932
Nickel	Axel Cronstedt	Sweden	1751
Nitrogen	Daniel Rutherford	England	1772
Oxygen	Joseph Priestly	England	1772
	C.W. Scheele	Sweden	
Ozone	Christian Schonbein	Germany	1839
Pluto (Planet)	Clyde Tombaugh	U.S.A	1930
Plutonium	G.T. Seaborg	U.S.A	1940
Proton	Ernest Rutherford	England	1919
Quantum Theory	Max Planck	Germany	1900
Radioactivity	Antoine Bacquerel	France	1896
Radium	Pierre & Marie Curie	France	1898
Silicon	Jons Berzelius	Sweden	1824
Special theory of relativity	Albert Einstein	Switzerland	1905
Sun as centre of solar system	Copernicus	Poland	1543
Uranium	Martin Klaproth	Germany	1789
Uranus (Planet)	William Herschel	England	1781
X-rays	Wilhelm Roentgen	Germany	1895

General Knowledge

Name of Instrument	Used for
Altimeter	measuring altitude
Ammeter	measuring strength of an electric current
Anemometer	measuring the velocity of wind
Audiometer	measuring level of hearing
Barometer	measuring atmospheric pressure
Callipers	measuring the internal and external diameters of tubes
Calorimeter	measuring quantity of heat
Compass	finding out direction
Dynamo	converting mechanical energy into electrical energy
Galvanometer	detecting and determining the strength of small electric currents
Hydrometer	measuring specific gravity of a liquid
Hygrometer	measuring the humidity in the atmosphere
Lactometer	measuring the purity of milk
Manometer	measuring the gaseous pressure
Micrometer	measuring minute distances, angles, etc.
Microscope	seeing magnified view of very small objects
Photometer	measuring intensity of light from distant stars
Pyrometer	measuring high temperatures
Radar	detecting and finding the presence and location of moving objects like aircraft, missile, etc.
Radiometer	measuring the emission of radiant energy
Rain Gauge	measuring the amount of rainfall
Seismograph	measuring and recording the intensity and origin of earthquake shocks
Sextant	measuring altitude and angular distances between two objects or heavenly bodies
Spectrometer	measuring the refractive indices
Spherometer	measuring the curvature of spherical objects/surface
Sphygmomanometer	measuring blood pressure
Stethoscope	ascertaining the condition of heart and lungs by listening to their function
Stroboscope	viewing objects that are moving rapidly with a periodic motion as if they were at rest
Tachometer	measuring the rate of revolution or angular speed of a revolving shaft
Telescope	viewing magnified images of distant objects
Thermocouple	measuring the temperature inside furnaces and jet engines
Thermometer	measuring human body temperature
Thermostat	regulating constant temperature
Ultrasonoscope	measuring utrasonic sounds
Viscometer	measuring the viscosity of a fluid
Voltmeter	measuring potential difference between two points.

General Knowledge

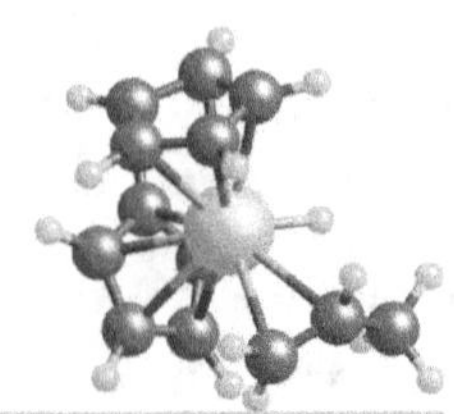

ELEMENTS

- An element may be defined as a substance which is made by same type of atoms and it can neither be broken into, nor built from two or more simpler substances by any known physical or chemical methods, e.g., copper, silver, hydrogen, carbon, oxygen, nitrogen, gold, iron etc.

COMPOUNDS

- A compound may be defined as a substance which contains two or more elements combined in some fixed proportion by weight and which can be decomposed into two or more elements by any suitable method.
- The properties of a compound are entirely different from those of the elements from which it is made.
- Some common examples of compounds are water, sugar, salt, aspirin, chloroform, alcohol and ether.

MIXTURES

- A material containing two or more elements or compounds in any proportion is a mixture.
- The components of a mixture can be separated by physical means like filtration, sublimation and distillation.

ATOMIC STRUCTURE

ATOM

- Atom is the smallest part of the element that takes part in a chemical reaction. Atom of an element can not be changed

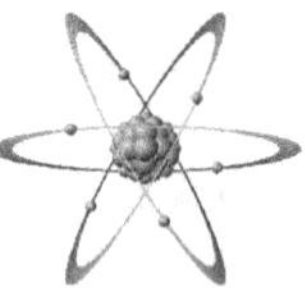

into that of another element by a chemical or physical means. It odes not exist in free state.

MOLECULE

- A molecule is the smallest part of an element or compound that is capable of existing independently.

ATOMIC WEIGHT (OR ATOMIC MASS)

- The atomic mass of an element is the number of times its atom is heavier than 1/12th of the mass of carbon (C^{12}) atom.
- The unit used to measure atomic mass called atomic mass unit, i.e., amu.

ELECTRON

- The electron is a fundamental particle of an atom which carries a unit negative charge. It was discovered by J.J. Thomson in 1897.

PROTON

- It is a fundamental particle of an atom carrying a unit positive charge. It was discovered by Rutherford and Goldstein in 1886.

NEUTRON

- It is a fundamental particle of an atom carrying no charge. It was discovered by Chadwick in 1932.

ISOTOPES

- The atoms of the same element having different mass numbers are called isotopes.

ISOBARS

- Elements having the same atomic mass but differ in atomic number are called isobars.

ISOTONES

- Elements having the same number of neutrons are called isotones.

OXIDATION AND REDUCTION

- Oxidation is a process in which a substance adds on oxygen or loses hydrogen. In modern terms, oxidation is the process in which a substance loses electrons.
- Reduction is a process in which a substance adds on hydrogen or loses oxygen. In modern terms, reduction is the process in which a substance gains electrons.
- Oxidation and reduction always occur simultaneously. If one substance is oxidised, another is reduced. The reaction in which this oxidation-reduction process occurs is called a redox reaction.
- Oxidising agents are substances which bring about the oxidation of other substances, e.g., Potassium Permanganate, Potassium Dichromate, Nitric Acid, Hydrogen Peroxide, etc.
- Reducing agents are substances which bring about the reduction of other substances, e.g., hydrogen sulphide, hydrogen, carbon, sulphur dioxide, etc.

ACIDS, BASES AND SALTS

ACID

- An acid is any compound that can react with a  base to form a salt, the hydrogen of the acid being replaced by positive metallic ion. According to modern theory, an acid is a compound which yields hydrogen ions (protons) to a base in a chemical reaction. In a water solution, an acid tastes sour, turns blue litmus red and produces free hydrogen ions.

Acid	Sources
Citric Acid	Lemons or Oranges (Citrus Fruits)
Lactic acid	Sour milk
Tartaric acid	Grapes
Acetic acid	Vinegar
Maleic acid	Apples
Oxalic acid	Tomato
Formic acid	Red ants

BASES

- Such compounds which gives salt and water with acid known as bases. Bitter in taste, turns red litmus paper into blue, contains replaceable hydroxyl group.
- Some important bases are sodium hydroxide, potassium hydroxide, sodium carbonate and ammonium hydroxide.
- All alkalies are bases but all bases are not alkalies because all bases are not soluble in water.

SALTS

- Salts are ionic compounds containing a positive ion (cation) and a negative ion (anion).
- When an acid reacts with a base, a salt and water are formed. This reaction is called neutralization since the acid and base neutralize each other's effect.

ELECTROLYSIS

- The process of decomposition of an electrolyte by the passage of an electric current through its molten state or its aqueous solution is called electrolysis.
- Device through which electric current is passed known as electrodes.

METALLURGY

- Metals occur in nature, in the native (in free state) as well as in the combined state.
- Naturally occurring materials containing metals are called minerals.
- A mineral from which a given metal is obtained economically is called an ore.

General Knowledge

- The process of extraction of a metal in a pure state on a large scale from its ore by Physical and Chemical means is called metallurgy.
- The rocky and siliceous matter that associated with the ore is known as gangue.
- Substance that is added to ore to remove the gangue is known as flux.
- The process of removal of gangue from the ore is known as concentration.
- Calcination is the heating of the ore in the absence of air. This method is employed for obtaining the metal oxides from carbonates and hydroxides.
- Roasting is the heating of the ore in the presence of air. On roasting, part of the ore is oxidised to form an oxide. This oxide is then reduced to the metal.
- The industrial reduction process for obtaining metal from the treated ore is called smelting.

AMALGUM

- An alloy in which one of the component metals is mercury is known as amalgum.

IRON AND STEEL

- Iron is extracted from its ores by the blast furnace process.
- Iron obtained from blast furnace is called pig iron or cast iron containing about 5% carbon.
- Pure iron is called wrought iron which does not contain carbon more than 0.2%, or any other impurities or constituents.
- Steel contains 0.25% – 2% carbon and varying amounts of other elements.

CARBON AND ITS COMPOUNDS

ALLOTROPY

- Such substances which having the same chemical properties, but differ in physical properties, known as allotropes and this property is called allotropy.

DIAMOND

- Diamond is the purest form of carbon.
- It is non-conductor of heat and electricity.
- It is the hardest natural substance.
- It burns in air at 900°C and gives out CO_2.

GRAPHITE (BLACK LEAD)

- It is good conductor of heat and electricity.
- Graphite is used in making lead pencils.
- Graphite is also used as electrodes, lubricant, moderators, electrotyping and carbon arc.

AMORPHOUS FORMS OF CARBON

1. Wood Charcoal – Obtained from wood
2. Sugar Charcoal – Obtained from cane sugar
3. Bone or Animal Charcoal – Obtained from animal bones
4. Coke Charcoal – Obtained from coal

CARBON MONOXIDE (CO)

- Carbon monoxide is an active poison and is very dangerous as it is a colourless and odourless gas and cannot, therefore, be easily detected.
- The extremely poisonous nature of carbon monoxide is a result of its combining with the haemoglobin of the blood to form carboxyhaemoglobin, which is not decompassed by any of the processes in the body.

HYDROCARBONS

- Compounds of carbon and hydrogen are called hydrocarbon.
- A natural source of hydrocarbon is petroleum obtained from sedimentary rocks.
- Compounds having the same molecular formula but differ in properties due to different structural formula known as isomers and this property is called isomerism.

Saturated Hydrocarbons (Alkanes)

- Containing single covalent bonds only.
- Such compounds are, in general, called alkanes for instance, Methane, Ethane, Propane, Butane.

Unsaturated Hydrocarbons

- Containing multiple bonds.
- Compounds with double bonds are called alkenes, e.g. ethylene, propyene etc and triple bond containing compounds are called alkynes, e.g. acetylene, propyne etc.
- Benzene is an unsaturated cyclic hydrocarbon with the structure.
- Compounds derived from benzene are called aromatic compounds.

FUELS

Solid Fuels

- These contain carbon and, during combustion, form mainly carbon dioxide and carbon monoxide with a large amount of heat.
- Examples of solid fuels are wood, coal, coke and paraffin wax.

Liquid Fuels

- These are basically mixtures of several hydrocarbons. During combustion, they form carbon dioxide and water.
- Liquid fuels are obtained as different fractions during the distillation of petroleum.
- Examples of liquid fuels are kerosene oil, petrol, diesel oil and alcohol.

Gaseous Fuels

- Gaseous fuels do not leave ash on burning and have high content of heat.
- The main gaseous fuels are liquefied petroleum gas (LPG, mainly a mixture of propane and butane and used in homes for cooking, water gas ($CO + H_2$), producer gas ($CO + N_2$), coal gas (mixture of hydrogen, methane ethylene, carbon monoxide, nitrogen, oxygen and carbon dioxide) and natural gas (mixture of methane, ethane, propane and butane with traces of higher hydrocarbons obtained from oil well, above petroleum).

PETROLEUM AND NATURAL GAS

- Natural gas contains about 80% methane and 10% ethane, the remaining 10% being a mixture of higher gaseous hydrocarbons.
- Compressed Natural Gas (CNG) is natural gas filled in cylinders under high pressure.
- The quality of petrol for use in car engines is denoted by their anti-knock properties.
- To increase octane number, tetra ethyl lead (TEL) is added to petrol.

HEAVY WATER

- Chemically heavy water is deuterium oxide.
- Heavy water is used in nuclear reactors as a moderator because it slows the fast moving neutrons.

Hard and Soft Water

- Water which produces lather with soap solution readily is called soft water.
- Water which does not produce lather with soap solution readily is called hard water.
- The hardness of water is due to presence of the bicarbonates, chlorides and sulphates of calcium and magnesium.
- Temporary hardness of water is due to the presence of bicarbonates of calcium and magnesium.
- Permanent hardness of water is due to presence of bicarbonates of calcium and magnesium.

GLASS

- Ordinary glass is solid mixture of silica, sodium silicate and calcium silicate.
- Soft glass is a soda-lime silicate glass. It melts at low temperature. It is used in manufacturing of bottles, test tubes etc.
- Hard glass is potash lime silicate and melts at high temperature in comparison to soft glass and is used in manufacturing of flask etc.

General Knowledge

- Flint glass is a lead potash silicate and is used in manufacturing of prism and lens optical instruments.
- Pyrex glass is a mixture of sodium aluminium borosilicates. It is used in manufacturing of high quality equipments in laboratory because it does not melt at very high temperature.
- Safety glass is prepared by placing a layer of transparent plastic glass between two layers of glass by means of a suitable adhesive. It is used in making wind screen of automobiles, aeroplanes, trains etc.

CEMENT

- The approximate composition of Portland cement is:
  1. Calcium Oxide   → 62%
  2. Silica   → 22%
  3. Alumina   → 7.5%
  4. Magnesia   → 2.5%
  5. Ferric Oxide   → 2.5%
- A small amount of gypsum is added to slow down the setting of cement.
- Cement containing excess amount of lime cracks during setting while cement containing less amount of lime is weak in strength.
- Cement containing no iron is white but hard to burn.

POLYMERS AND PLASTICS

- A polymer is a large molecule, built up from many hundreds of thousands of small unit called monomeric units or monomers.
- The process of formation of polymers from monomers is called polymerization.
- Plastics are cross-linked polymers and very tough.
- Some examples of plastics are — Celluloid, Bakelite and Vinyl Plastics.

RUBBER

- Natural and Synthetic rubbers are examples of polymers.
- Natural rubber is isomer of isoprene.
- When the natural rubber is heated along with sulphur called vulcanisation. The resulting rubber is elastic, hard and strong.
- Synthetic rubbers are made by polymerisation of chloroprene, styrene and butadiene mixtures and isobutylene.

SOAPS

- The soaps are sodium salts of higher fatty acids. They are useful only in soft water as they form an insoluble precipitate in hard water. This precipitate consists of salts of calcium and magnesium of higher fatty acids. No lather or emulsion is formed and washing is not possible.

☞ **Some Importants Alloys**

Alloys	Composition
Brass	Cu, Zn
Bronze	Cu, Sn
Gun metal	Cu, Sn, Zn
Bel metal	Cu, Sn
German silver	Cu, Zn, Ni
Dutch metal	Cu, Zn
Aluminium	Al, Cu
Nichrome	Ni, Fe, Cr, Mn
Chromium steel	Cr, C, Fe

☞ **Chemical Formulae, Commercial name of chemical compounds:**

Commercial Name	Chemical Compounds	Chemical formulae
Common salt	Sodium chloride	$NaCl$
Baking soda	Sodium bicarbonate	$NaHCO_3$
Washing soda	Sodium carbonate	$Na2CO_3 . 10H_2O$
Caustic soda	Sodium hydroxide	$NaOH$
Chilli salt peter	Sodium nitrate	$NaNO_3$
Soda ash	Sodium carbonate	Na_2CO_3
Hypo	Sodium thiosulphate	$Na_2S_2O_3 . 5H_2O$

BIOLOGY

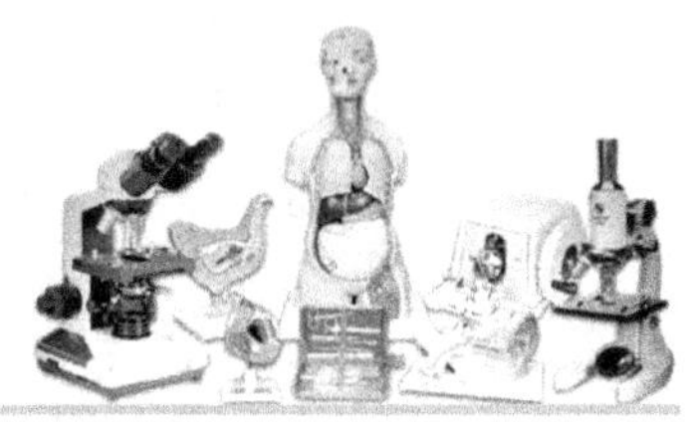

BRANCHES OF BIOLOGY

(a) **Anthropology:** Deals with the scientific study of man and the mankind.

(b) **Agronomy:** Deals with the management of farms and science of crop production.

(c) **Apiculture:** Deals with the process of bee keeping for commercial purposes.

(d) **Entomology:** Deals with the structure, habits and classification of insects.

(e) **Eugenics:** Deals with improving the human race.

(f) **Pathology:** Deals with the nature of disease, their causes, symptoms, effects, their cure and control.

(g) **Physiotherapy:** Deals with the treatment of diseases, body weakness or defects with the help of massage and exercise etc.

(h) **Sericulture:** Deals with the production of raw silk from silkworm.

(i) **Pharmacology:** Deals with the knowledge and manufacture of drugs.

(j) **Occupational therapy:** Deals with treating the physically handicapped or injured persons through exercise etc.

(k) **Psychology:** Deals with the study of human mind, its behaviour and mental qualities.

(l) **DNA finger printing:** Technique to help identify a person on the basis of genes.

ANIMALS/PLANTS

- The organisms that closely resemble one another are placed in one group, the groups which have similarities are combined together into larger groups, and these into still larger ones. The most inclusive category is kingdom. Other major categories, in descending order are: phylum, class, order, family, genus, and species. Man belongs to Animal kingdom, chordata division or phylum, Mammalia class, Primates order, Hominidae family, Homogenus and Sapiens species.

CELL THEORY

- Cell is the basic unit of structure of all living organisms. According to the cell theory, all organism are composed of cells and cell products and growth and development results from the division and differentiation of cells.

- Cells membrane surrounds all living cells.

- Nucleus is the most important cell orgallelle which controls and coordinates all cell activities and also concerned with the transmission of heredity characters.

- Mitochondria, ribosomes, Iysosomes and dictyosomes are present in plant and animal cells.

- Only plant cells have cell wall, chloroplast and vacuole.

- Viruses constitute a difficulty since in many ways they are intermediate between living and dead matter.

- The cell is said to be made up of a substance called Protoplasm which has two main constituents cytoplasm and nucleus, and is bounded by a cell membrane on outside.

- Cells take up the raw materials for metabolism through the cell membrane from extracellular fluid surrounding them.

General Knowledge

- Cytoplasm inside is responsible for maintaining the internal distribution of organelles and also for free cell movements.
- Mitochondria inside provides energy for reactions inside the cell. Ribosomes are responsible for the synthesis of proteins.
- The Endoplasmic Reticulum helps in addition of other sugar units to proteins and their transportation to other parts of the cell.

FOOD

- It is a nutritive substance taken by an organism for growth, work, repair and maintaining life processes. It provides energy to do work and maintain body heat, provides materials for the growth of the body, makes necessary materials for reproduction and provides materials for the repair of damaged cells and tissues of our body.
- **Carbohydrates:** For a normal person, 400 to 500 gms of carbohydrates are required daily but for sportspersons, growing children and nursing mothers, it is on higher side.
- **Proteins:** They are complex organic compounds made up of carbon, hydrogen, oxygen and nitrogen. The building blocks of Protein are Amino acids and there are large number of amino acids.
- Proteins are essential for the growth of children and teenagers, and for maintenance and making good the wear and tear of the body tissues in adults.
- An adult needs about 1 gm of protein per kg of body weight.
- **Fats:** They are esters of long chain fatty acids and an alcohol called glycerol. Fats also contain atoms of carbon, hydrogen and oxygen.
- The main function of fats in the body is to provide a steady source of energy and for this purpose, they are deposited within the body.
- One gm of fat gives 37 kilojoules of energy which is more than double of that given by carbohydrates.
- Fats, the richest source of energy to our body, can be stored in the body for subsequent use. Fats, soluble in organic solvents and insoluble in water, also supply fat-soluble vitamins to our body.
- **Minerals:** Some of the important minerals needed by our body are — iron, iodine, calcium, phosphorus, sodium, potassium, zinc, copper, magnesium, chloride, fluoride and sulphur.
- We get most of the minerals in combined form from plant sources. Deficiency of these minerals causes many diseases.
- **Energy Requirements:** The energy requirement of a body varies according to age, sex, lifestyle, occupation, climate and special situations like pregnancy and lactation.

Age	Energy requirements
5 years	6000 kJ per day
11 years	9000 kJ per day
18 years	11000 kJ per day
Adult (normal work)	9600 kJ per day
Adult (heavy work)	12000 kJ per day
Adult (very heavy work)	16000 kJ per day

- **Vitamins:** They act as catalysts in certain chemical reactions of metabolism in our body.
- They don't provide energy to our body nor form body tissues.
- More than 15 types of vitamins are known and only 2 vitamins — D and K can be formed in our body.

Vitamin	Necessity	Source
Vitamin A	For maintaining healthy eyesight, normal skin and hair	Cod liver oil, fish, eggs, milk, carrot, leafy vegetables.
Vitamin B_1	For growth, carbohydrate metabolism, functioning of heart, nerves and muscles.	Milk, soya-food, meat, whole cereals, green vegetables.
Vitamin C	For keeping teeth, gums and joints healthy, for increasing resistance of body to infection	Citrus fruits, guava, tomatoes.
Vitamin D	For normal growth of bones and teeth	Milk, eggs, butter, cod liver oil, sun light.
Vitamin E	For normal reproduction, functioning of muscles and protection of liver	Green leafy vegetables, milk, butter, tomato.
Vitamin K	For normal clotting of blood and normal functioning of liver	Green leafy vegetables, soyabean, tomato.

- **Roughage:** Though it does not provide any energy to the body, yet keeps the digestive system in order, by helping in retaining water in the body and preserving constitution.
- The main source of roughage are salads, cabbage, corn cob, porridge, vegetables and fruits with stems.

DISEASES

COMMUNICABLE DISEASES

- They are the diseases which can be transmitted from reservoirs of infection or infected person to the healthy but susceptible persons.
- The disease causing agent or the pathogen can be transmitted directly or indirectly.

DEFICIENCY DISEASES

- These occur due to deficiency of some nutrients in the diet or some hormone due to hypo activity or damage to endocrine glands.

Diet Deficiency	Disease
Protein	Kwashiorkor
Protein-energy malnutrition	Marasmus
Vitamin A	Night-blindness, Xerophthalmia
Vitamin B_1	Beri-Beri
Vitamin B_2	Cheilosis
Vitamin B_5	Pellagra
Vitamin C	Scurvy
Vitamin D	Rickets (in children), (in adult) Osteomalacia
Vitamin K	Hypothrombinemia
Iron	Anaemia
Iodine	Goitre
Fluoride	Dental caries
Calcium and phosphorus	Affects formation of bones and teeth

Hormone Deficiency	Disease
Insulin	Diabetes
Thyroxine	Cretinism (child), Goitre
STH	Dwarfism, Gigantism

ALLERGIC DISEASE

- In these diseases, body becomes hypersensitive to some foreign agents, allergens, which cause inflammation when come in contact with the body or enter inside the body.
- Foreign agents can be dust, pollens, certain-foods, serum, certain drugs or fabrics.
- The unfavourable response of the body to allergens is called allergic reaction. Asthma and hay fever are allergic diseases.

General Knowledge

BACTERIAL DISEASES

- Bacteria are minute organisms which are known to cause a number of diseases:

Disease	Incubation period	Spread through
Tuberculosis	2-10 weeks	Air-borne, droplet infection
Diptheria	2-6 days	Air-borne droplet infection
Cholera	6 hours to 2-3 days	Contaminated food and water. House flies are the vectors
Leprosy	Upto 5 years	Prolonged and intimate contact
Whopping cough	7-14 days	Droplet infection
Tetanus	3-21 days	Entry of cysts through any wound made by sharp object, dog bite or fall on the road
Typhoid	1-3 weeks	Directed and Contact
Plague	2-6 days	Rats and bed-bugs transmit the germs
Pneumonia	1-3 days	Air-borne

VIRAL DISEASES

Disease	Incubation period	Spread through
Chicken-pox	12-20 days	Direct contact with infected persons or infected objects
Smallpox	12 days	Droplet infection
Poliomyalitis	7-14 days	Direct and oral
Measles	10 days	Droplet infection
Mumps	12-26 days	Droplet infection
Rabies	1-3 months	Bite of rabied animal like dogs, monkeys, cates
Influenza	24-28 hours	Air-borne

DISEASES CAUSED BY PROTOZOA

- Amoebiasis (Amoebic dysentery), Malaria, Kala-azar, Trypanosomiasis and Giardiasis are main diseases caused by Protozoans.
- Malaria is a parasitic infection.

PARTS OF PLANTS

ROOTS

- Root is an underground cylindrical part of the plant which develops from radicle and grows vertically down into the soil.
- The primary functions of the root is to fix the plant firmly with the soil and to absorb water and mineral nutrients.
- In some plants, roots help in synthesis of food, respiration, storing food, helping the weak stem climb and vegetative reproduction.
- Nodulated roots of Gram, Groundnut, Beans, etc. have nitrogen fixing bacteria.

STEM

- Stem is the main axis of plants. It develops from plumule of embryo, grows in the upward direction, towards the sun.
- Its main function is to conduct water, mineral and food material, to produce and support of leaves and reproductive structure.

LEAF

- Leaves are the food manufacturing organs of the plant.
- Green leaves contain chlorophyll which is responsible for manufacturing food.
- Loss of water takes place from leaf surface, called transpiration, which creates tension needed for ascent of food, water and nutrients.
- Through leaves exchange of gases between the environment and the plant takes place.
- In some plants, leaves store food and water, protect from grazing animals, help in vegetative reproduction, help in climbing the plants with weak stem.

Photosynthesis

- It is the only process on Earth by which solar energy is trapped by autotrophic organisms and converted into food.

- Inorganic compounds carbon dioxide and water form carbohydrates in the presence of chlorophyll and sunlight with liberation of oxygen.

SYSTEM OF HUMAN BODY

DIGESTIVE SYSTEM

- The digestive system consists of alimentary canal and digestive glands. Alimentary canal is about 8-10 meters long tube of varying diameter. Food is taken in through mouth.
- The tongue helps in ingestion, chewing, tasting and swallowing of food and mixing of food and saliva.
- Salivary glands secret saliva which helps in digestion of starch. Gastric glands present in the mucosa of the stomach, provide acidic medium for the food digestion.
- Liver, the largest sized, reddish brown gland of body, secrets bile. Liver is present in the right upper part of the abdomen. The bile secreted by the liver is stored in gall bladder. It helps in the emulsification and digestion of fats.
- Pancreas is the second largest gland in human body and secretes pancreatic juices. Intestine also secret juices.

RESPIRATORY SYSTEM

- Oxygen is needed for the oxidation and expelling of carbon dioxide is necessary to avoid its-accumulation. This process of exchange of gases between the environment and the body, is called respiration.
- In some unicellular organisms like aerobic bacteria, amoeba, hydra, etc. there is direct exchange of gases between the carbon dioxide of the body and oxygen of water.
- There is no blood for transport of gases. However, in larger and complex form of animals, specialised respiratory organs are developed.

- Amphibians respire through skin, fishes through gills and mammals birds and reptiles through lungs.
- A normal adult inspires or expires about 500 ml of gas with each breath and about 72 breathes per minutes.

CIRCULATORY SYSTEM

- Main components of the circulatory system are heart, blood vessels and blood.
- Heart is a thick, muscular, contractile and automatic pumping organ. In birds and mammals, heart is divided into four chambers.
- Arteries are thick walled blood vessels which always carry the blood away from the heart to various body parts.
- Veins are thin walled blood vessels which always carry the blood from various parts generally to the heart.
- In an adult healthy person, the normal rate of heart beat at rest is about 70-72 times per minute.

BLOOD

- It is red, opaque, somewhat sticky and viscous fluid in the body of animals.
- It is slightly alkaline (pH = 7.4), heavier than water (sp gr = 1.05) and five times more viscous than distilled water.
- Blood forms 6 to 10% of the body weight.
- An adult, on average, has about 6.8 litres of blood.
- Blood contains plasma and blood corpuscles with the former occupying 55-60% of the volume.
- Plasma transports food components, metabolic wastes and hormones; keeps constant level of pH of blood, maintains body temperature and helps in blood clotting.
- Erythrocytes or red blood corpuscles (RBCs), leukocytes or white blood corpuscles (WBCs) and blood platelets are other parts of the blood.

General Knowledge

- Due to the presence of iron containing pigment haemoglobin, RBCs are red in colour. The RBCs are crucial for exchange of oxygen and carbon dioxide. WBCs are nucleated and non-pigmented cells. They are larger in size than RBCs but far less in number (1 : 600).
- WBCs play an important role in immune system of the body. Blood platelets cause the coagulation of blood and clot formation to prevent excessive bleeding.
- Human blood is divided into four main Groups—A, B, AB and O.
- The plasma of Group A blood contains an anti-B factor and vice-versa, so that people of Groups A and B cannot accept each other's blood.
- Group AB contains neither anti-A nor anti-B factor and people with this group can receive transfusions from both but can give to neither.
- Group O contains both anti-A and anti-B and can receive blood only from Group O but can donate blood to all Groups. Group O is called universal donor because they can donate to all the Groups.
- Group AB is called universal acceptor because they can accept blood from all Groups.

SKELETON SYSTEM

- The frame or the hard structure of the human body is composed from the bones and the organs of making such frame are called skeleton system.

Bones

- Bone is the hardest tissue of the body and form the largest section of the body weight.
- Bones contain organic as well as inorganic matters. With advancing age, the inorganic matter's share increases, causing the bones to become more brittle.
- Long bones such as humerus and femur are hollow while small bones are solid.

EXCRETORY SYSTEM

- In men, excretory system is formed of one pair of kidneys, one pair of ureters, a urinary bladder and a urethra. Kidney is about 10 cm long, bean shaped, dark-red and slightly flattened structure.
- Sweet glands, oil glands, lungs and liver also act as additional excretory organ.
- In case of kidney failure, a man can treated by hemodialysis or transplantation of a kidney from a donor's body.

NERVOUS SYSTEM

- The system which controls and coordinates the body functions, retains memory and receives and sends signals, is called the nervous system.
- The nervous system comprises brain, spinal cord, nerves and nerve fibres.
- Human brain weighs about 1200 to 1400 gm. Main parts of the brain are cerebrum, cerebellum and medulla oblongata.
- Cerebrum controls voluntary function and is site of intelligence, will power, emotions, etc.
- Cerebellum controls involuntary functions like heart beat, respiration, etc.
- Spinal cord is about 45 cm long and about 35 gm in weight. It conducts impulses to and from the brain and controls reflex actions of the body.
- Various cranial (arising from of ending into brain) and spinal nerves (arising from spinal cord) control smell, vision, movements of body parts, taste and hearing.

REPRODUCTION SYSTEM

- In this type of reproduction, there is formation and fusion of sex cells, called gametes.

General Knowledge

- Organism develops from the zygote through embryo formation.
- It generally involves two parents — male and female.
- The offsprings are different from the parent as variations appear due to new combinations of genes. So, it plays an important role in evolution.
- All higher plants and animals reproduce sexually.

CHROMOSOMES

- Plants and animals have fixed number of chromosomes per cell.
- Genes are located on chromosomes and are responsible for transfer of characteristics from one cell to the next either in the same organism or from parents to offspring.
- Man has 23 pairs of chromosomes, of which one pair is sex chromosomes.
- Males child inherits X chromosomes from the female parent and Y from the male parent.
- Female child receives a X chromosome each from either of its parents.
- Mendel was the first scientist to explain transmission of units from reproductive cells of the parents to the off-springs.

CLONING

- It is the process of producing genetically identical copies of a biological material, starting from a single cell. The original genes are transplanted and thus one can produce organisms of known and desirable characteristics.

GENETIC ENGINEERING

- It is the method of artificial synthesis of new genes and their subsequent transplantation or methods of correcting the defective genes.
- It has helped in producing plants and animals with specific characters.
- So, crippling hereditary diseases can also be cured like hemophilia etc.

DNA FINGERPRINTING

- It consists of examining repetitive DNA in the genome for variations in the length of restriction fragments.
- Every individual has his own pattern, so that fingerprinting can match blood to a particular person, and patterns are inherited from parent to child, allowing the method to identify relationships between individuals.

IN-VITRO FERTILIZATION

- When a sperm and an egg are made to fertilize outside a living body (usually a test tube), it is called in-vitro fertilization.
- This process has been used to impregnate several females who could not do so through natural means.

☞ DISEASES AND THE PARTS OF BODY THEY AFFECT

Disease	Part of body affected
AIDS	Immune system of body
Arthritis	Inflammation of joints
Asthma	Lungs
Cataract	Eyes
Conjunctivitis	Eyes
Diabetes	Pancreas
Diphtheria	Throat
Glaucoma	Eyes
Eczema	Skin
Goitre	Front of the neck (due to enlargement of thyroid gland)
Gout	Joints of bone

Disease	Part of body affected
Jaundice	Liver
Meningitis	Brain or spinal cord
Pleurisy	Pleura (inflammation of)
Polio	motor neurons
Pneumonia	Lungs
Pyorrhoea	Sockets of teeth
Tuberculosis	Lungs
Typhoid	Intestine
Malaria	Spleen
Leukaemia	Blood
Rickets	Bones

General Knowledge

SPACE RESEARCH

- Indian Space Research Organisation (ISRO) came into existence in 1969. However, in India, space programme was formally organised in 1972 with the setting up of Space Commission and Department of Space (DoS). The primary objective of India's space programme is to develop satellites, launch vehicles and associated ground-systems.

INDIAN SATELLITES IN SPACE

1. **Aryabhatta:** Indian Space Research Organisation (ISRO) with the assistance of former USSR built its first satellite in 1975 and launched it successfully into space on April 19, 1975 from a cosmodrome situated there. India became the eleventh country in the world to orbit satellites. The first satellite was named Aryabhatta after the great Indian astronomer and mathematician of the 5th century.

2. **Bhaskara I:** India's second satellite Bhaskara I named after Bhaskaras, two ancient Indian astronomers and mathematicians, born in the 6th and 12th centuries, respectively, was also launched from a Soviet cosmodrome on June 7, 1979.

3. **Rohini-I:** India's third satellite Rohini-I was launched into space on August 10, 1979 by an Indian manufactured rocket SLV-3 from Sriharikota.

4. **Rohini-II:** Rohini-II was the fourth Indian satellite. It was put into orbit like its predecessor Rohini-I. It was launched on July 18, 1980.

5. **APPLE:** India's fifth satellite APPLE was launched aboard the European Space Agency's Ariane Launch Vehicle from Kourou in French Guyana on June 19, 1981. It was India's first ever geo-synchronous satellite.

6. **Bhaskara-II:** India's sixth satellite Bhaskara-II—an earth observation satellite—was launched from Soviet cosmodrome Volgograd on November 20, 1981.

7. **INSAT-1A:** India's seventh and most important satellite INSAT-1A was launched from Cape Canaveral on April 10, 1982. It was India's first multipurpose domestic satellite. India successfully launched a series of INSAT satellites.

☞ **First in Space**

✶ First creator of rules regarding space research	Isaac Newton
✶ First artificial satellite launched in space	Sputnik-1 (1957)
✶ First living being sent in space	Louika (a dog)
✶ Firstever manned spacecraft	Vostok-I
✶ First man in space	Yuri Gagarin U.S.S.R. (1961)
✶ First woman in space	Valentina Tereshkova U.S.S.R. (June 1963)
✶ First man who moved in space out of the spacecraft	Alexi Livonov U.S.S.R. (June 1965)
✶ First person to land on moon	Neil Armstrong, America (21st July, 1969)

 **General Knowledge**

* First fourwheeled carriage without human being on moon — Leunokhev-I U.S.S.R. (1970)
* First space lab in orbit — Skylab (America, 1973)
* First space shuttle — Columbia (America, 1981)
* First Indian (man) in space — Squadron leader—Rakesh Sharma (13th April, 1984)
* First Indian (Woman) in space — Kalpana Chawla (19th Nov., 1997)
* First American woman in space — Sailyride (1983)
* First spacecraft on Mars — Pathfinder (6 July, 1997)
* First woman who lead spacecraft — Allin Collis (America)
* First spacecraft without man — Shenzoo, China (20th Nov. 1999)

☞ Indian Space Programme : At a Glance

Satellite	Date	Type	Launch Vehicle	Result
Aryabhatta	19-04-75	Scientific	Cosmos	successful
Bhaskara I	07-06-79	Geosurvey	Cosmos	successful
Rohini	10-08-79	Geosurvey	S.L.V.3	unsuccessful
Rohini D-1	18-07-80	Geosurvey	S.L.V.3	successful
Rohini	31-05-81	Scientific	S.L.V.3	successful
Apple	19-06-81	Communication	Ariane	successful
Bhaskara II	20-11-81	Geosurvey	Cosonos	successful
INSAT-1A	10-04-82	Multipurpose	Delta	unsuccessful
Rohini	17-04-83	Scientific	S.L.V.3	successful
INSAT-1B	30-08-83	Multipurpose	Space Shuttle	successful
SROSS I	24-03-87	Technical	ASLV-D1	unsuccessful
IRS-1A	17-03-88	Remote sensing	Vostok	successful
SROSS II	17-07-88	Technical	ASLV-D2	unsuccessful
INSAT-1C	21-07-88	Multipurpose	Ariane-4	unsuccessful
INSAT-1D	12-06-90	Multipurpose	Delta	successful
IRS-1B	29-08-91	Remote sensing	Vostok	successful
INSAT-2A	10-07-92	Multipurpose	Ariane	successful
INSAT-2B	23-07-93	Multipurpose	Ariane	successful
IRS-P1	20-09-93	Remote sensing	PSLV-D1	unsuccessful
SROSS-4	04-05-94	Scientific	ASLV-D3	successful
IRS-P2	15-10-94	Remote sensing	PSLV-D2	successful
INSAT-2C	07-12-95	Telecom	Ariane-4	successful
IRS-1C	28-12-95	Remote sensing	PSLV-D3	successful
IRS-P3	20-03-96	Remote sensing	PSLV-D3	successful
INSAT-2D	20-04-97	Telecom	Ariane	unsuccessful
IRS-ID	29-09-97	Remote sensing	PSLV	successful

General Knowledge

Satellite	Date	Type	Launch Vehicle	Result
G-SAT-1	18-04-2001	Multipurpose	GSLV-D	successful
INSAT-3C	24-01-2002	Communication	Ariane-4	successful
INSAT-3A	10-04-2003	Multipurpose	Ariane-5	successful
INSAT-3E	28-09-2003	Communication	Ariane-5	successful
CARTOSAT-1 & HAMSAT	05-05-2005	Maping and Communication	PSLV-C6	successful
INSAT-4A	22-12-2005	Communication	Ariane-5	successful
INSAT-4CR	02-09-2007	Communication	GSLV-Fo4	successful
CARTOSAT-2A	28-04-2008	Communication	PSLV-C9	successful
Chandrayaan-I	22-10-2008	Maping and Scientific	PSLV-C11	successful
RISAT-2 & ANUSAT	20-04-2009	Maping and Communication	PSLV-C12	successful
Oceansat-2	24-09-2009	Remote Sensing	PSLV-C14	successful
CARTOSAT-2B	12-07-2010	Communication	PSLV-C15	successful
RESOURCESAT-2	20-04-2011	Remote Sensing	PSLV-C16	successful
GSAT-8	21-05-2011	Communication	Ariane-5	successful
RISAT-1	26-04-2012	Remote Sensing	PSLV-C19	successful
Spot-6	09-09-2012	Remote Sensing	PSLV-C21	successful
Saral	25-02-2013	Scientific	PSLV-C20	successful
GSAT-7	30-08-2013	Defence	Ariane-5	successful
Mangalyan	05-11-2013	Maping and Scientific	PSLV-C25	successful
GSAT-14	05-01-2014	Communication	GSLV-D5	successful
IRNSS-1B	04-04-2014	Maping and Scientific	PSLV-C24	successful
Spot-7	30-06-2014	Remote Sensing	PSLV-C23	successful
GSAT-16	07-12-2014	Communication	Ariane-5	successful
IRNSS-1D	28-03-2015	Mapping and Scientific	PSLV-C27	successful
DMC3	10-07-2015	Mapping and Scientific	PSLV-C28	successful
DMC3	10-07-2015	Mapping and Scientific	PSLV-C28	successful
GSAT-6	27-p08-2015	Communication	GSLV-D6	successful
Astrosat	28-09-2015	Mapping and Scientific	PSLV-C30	successful
TeLEOS-1 & others	16-12-2015	Mapping and Scientific	PSLV-C29	successful
IRNSS-1E	20-01-2016	Mapping and Scientific	PSLV-C31	successful
IRNSS-1G	28-04-2016	Mapping and Scientific	PSLV-C33	successful
CARTOSAT-2 & others	22-06-2016	Mapping and Scientific	PSLV-C34	successful
INSAT-3DR	08-09-2016	Meteorology	GSLV-F05	successful
SCATSAT-1 & others	26-09-2016	Multipurpose	PSLV-C35	successful
GSAT-18	06-10-2016	Communication	Ariane-5	successful
Resourcesat-2A	07-12-2016	Remote Sensing	PSLV-C36	successful
CARTOSAT-2	15-02-2017	Multipurpose	PSLV-C37	successful
CARTOSAT-2F	12-01-2018	Multipurpose	PSLV-C40	successful
GSAT-6A	29-03-2018	Communication	GSLV-F-08	successful
CARTOSAT-F	12-01-2019	Mapping and Scientific	PSLV-C40	successful
RISAT-2B	22-05-2019	Mapping and Scientific	PSLV-C46	successful
Chandrayaan-2	22-07-2019	Mapping and Scientific	GSLV-MK-III	successful

 General Knowledge

COMPUTER

- The computer is the system of that electronic device through which various informations are processed on the basis of a definite set of instructions called program and mathematical (numerical) and non-mathematical both types of informations are processed.
- The first mechanical computer was composed or fabricated by Blaise Pascal in 1642 and it is called Pascalene.
- But in 1833, Charles Babbage first time conceived an automatic calculator or computer.
- Charles Babbage is called the father of modern computer.
- Herman made an electronic tabulating machine based on punch cards which operates automatically.
- In 1937, first mechanical computer mark-I was fabricated by Howard Akeen.
- The most outstanding contribution in the development of modern computer goes to John Wan Newmaan who brought the 2nd revolution in the area of computer in 1951.
- He discovered EDVAC (Electronic Discrete Variable Automatic Computer) and utilised the stored program and the binary number system in the computer.

FUNCTIONS OF COMPUTER

- 1. Collection and composition (input) of datas;
  2. Storage of datas.
  3. Processing of datas.
  4. Retrieval or output of the proccessed informations and datas.

UNITS OF COMPUTER

- 1. Input unit.
  2. Central processing unit–CPU.
  3. External Memory unit.
  4. Output unit.
- The CPU of the computer is called brain of the computer and sometimes CPU is also called Micro Processor of the computer.
- The data is entered through the input unit in the computer and through the central processing unit with the help of External Memory Unit datas are arranged and processed.
- Ultimately by the output unit these datas or informations are issued or released.

PARTS OF COMPUTER

- **Monitor :** The monitor of the computer is like a television in which the picture appears in the form of doted points on the screen and these are called pixcels.
- **Hard Disc and Floppy Disc :** The Hard Disc is the permanent disc in the computers while the Floppy Disc is the disc utilised when datas or informations are to be transferred from one computer to another.
- **Mouse :** The mouse of the computer is like the remote control of TV through which computer is directly regulated or controlled without utilising the keyboard.
- **Printer :** The printer is a device which prints any documents or processed informations of the computer.

General Knowledge

SOME HIGH LEVEL LANGUAGES

1. **FORTRAN :** This language was developed for solving the mathematical formulae very quickly and conveniently.

2. **COBOL :** This language was developed for the commerical purposes. For the processing of this language a group of sentences is selected called paragraph and all paragraphs composed are called a section, while all sections composed are called a division.

3. **BASIC :** In basic a definite part of the prescribed instruction is only inserted in the computer.

4. **ALGOL :** This was basically fabricated and designed for the complex algebraic calculations.

5. **PASCAL :** It is an amplified and modified form of ALGOL.

6. **COMAL :** This computer language is used for the students of secondary level.

7. **LOGO :** This language is used for children and kids for drawing Graphic line diagrams.

8. **PROLOG :** This language is developed in 1973 in France and this language is used for Artificial Intelligence which is capable and equivalent to the logical program.

9. **FORTH :** This language was invented by Charles Mure which is frequently used in all types of the works in the computer.

COMPUTER VIRUS

- The computer virus is an electronic code which is used to abolish or erradicate the inclusive informations or programs of the computer.

- Some important computer viruses are Micheleanjalo, Dork Avangor, kilo, filip, Macmug, Scores, Casecade, Jeruslem, Date crime, Coloumbs crime, Internet virus, Pachcom, Pach EXE, COM-EXE, Marizuana, C-brain, bloody, Chenge Mungu and Desi etc.

COMPUTER NETWORKING

- There are two types of networkings which are usually occur—Local Area Networking (LAN) and Wide Area Networking (WAN).

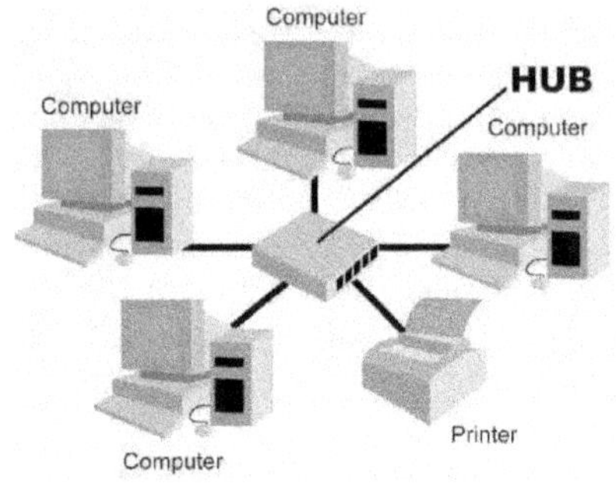

- By LAN all the computers of the same buildings are connected like the computers of university premises, computers of offices etc.

- By WAN all the comptuers of a large area are connected like the computers of all the offices of a city or town etc.

- In India a very large computer network namely INDONET has been installing through which all the main towns and cities has to be interlinked.

COMPUTER TERMINOLOGY

- **Bit :** The bit is a unit of measurement of the electronic data. One bit is either 0 or 1 but not both. On composing 8 bits, 1 byte is formed.

- **Bug :** The Bug is the error in the computer program or system and its eradication is called Debug.

- **Byte :** Total eight bits compose a byte. Thus 8 bits = 1 byte.

- **CD-ROM :** A CD like of music CD in which data can be stored substantially called CD-ROM. In a CD with comparison to floppy extremely more datas can be stored but one problem in it is that one time recorded data can not be deleted or modified.
- **Chip :** It is a thin slice on which by a special mechanism a circuit is designed which is normally made from Silicon.
- **Memory System :** The place where computer data and program are temporarily kept is called Memory system. Usually memory is implied from RAM.
- **Modem :** The device which converts digital signals into analogue signals and vice-versa is called Modem.
- **RAM :** It is Random Access Memory (a place) where datas to be processed are kept temporarily and it is unstable memory.
- **ROM :** It is Read Only Memory and it is stable or Non-valatile memory which doesn't ended after power off.
- **Scanner :** It is a device through which graphic image is transformed to digital image and the scanners are of usually two types one desktop and another hand operating.

PROGRAMING

- Computers perform phenomenal feats of calculation, but they do not do so in a complicated way.
- They actually carry out very simple operations, such as addition and subtraction.
- They achieve their fantastic computing power by carrying out these operations at incredible speed.
- The programme, or set of instructions for operating the computer, is therefore written as a sequence of very simple steps. (See box below) Several computer languages have been developed for different applications, including BASIC, COBOL, FORTRAN and PASCAL. Writing programmes is very skilled and time-consuming work.
- But for most typical computer applications ready-written programmes are available, called "packages".

☞ **How A Programme Works**

Without a programme to tell it what to do and how to do it, a computer is unable to function. If, for example, you wanted to know how many times the word 'the' appears in this paragraph, or in the whole book, it would not be enough merely to put the text into a computer and then ask it how many times the word appears. For the computer to accomplish the calculations it has to be told what to do in simple steps. The instructions might be:

1. Scan the text until a space followed by 'T' or 't' is found.
2. If the next letter is not 'h', go back to step 1.
3. If the letter is 'h', is the next letter 'e'?
4. If not, go back to step 1. If it is, go to step 5.
5. If 'e' is followed by a space, add 1 to the total.
6. Go back to step 1.

A full computer programme for this operation would need to be broken down into even more simple steps, but a series of such programmes could enable a computer to analyse any amount of text in great detail.

General Knowledge

General
KNOWLEDGE

☞ First in the World

✶ First Chinese visitor to India	*Fahien*
✶ First foreign invader of India	*Alexander, the Great (Greek)*
✶ First person to climb Mt. Everest	*Tenzing Norgay (India) and Edmund Hillary (New Zealand) (1953)*
✶ First atom bomb dropped at	*Hiroshima (Japan)*
✶ First man in the space	*Yuri Gagarin (former USSR)*
✶ First woman in the space	*Valentina Tereshkova (former USSR)*
✶ First person to walk in the space	*Alexei Leonov (former USSR)*
✶ First person to land on the moon	*Neil Armstrong (USA)*
✶ First and the only woman to have climbed Mt. Everest twice	*Santosh Yadav (Indian; May 12, 1992; May 10, 1993)*
✶ First person on Mt. Everest without oxygen	*Phu Dorjee (Indian; May 9, 1984)*
✶ First person to climb Mt. Everest twice	*Nawang Gombu*
✶ First person to climb Mt. Everest maximum times	*Chhewang Nima Sherpa (19 times)*
✶ First President of the USA	*George Washington*
✶ First woman Prime Minister	*Sirimavo Bandaranaike (Sri Lanka)*
✶ First person to swim across English Channel	*Mathew Webb*
✶ First woman to swim across English Channel	*Gertrude Caroline Ederle*
✶ First woman to climb Mt. Everest	*Junko Tabei (Japan)*
✶ First woman to climb Mt. Everest alone and without oxygen supplies	*Alison Hargreaves (Briton: May 13, 1995)*
✶ First Aeroplane to fly around the world without refuelling	*Voyager (Dec. 1986)*
✶ First test-tube Baby	*Louise Brown (UK; 1978)*
✶ First all-talking Film	*Jaz Singer (1927)*
✶ First Secretary-General of the UN	*Trygve Lie (Norway: 1946-53)*
✶ First woman President of the UN General Assembly	*Vijayalakshmi Pandit (India: 1953)*
✶ First woman to reach North Pole	*Ann Bancroft (1986)*
✶ First person to reach North Pole	*Robert Peary*
✶ First person to reach South Pole	*Amundsen (1911)*
✶ First woman to command Spacecraft in Space	*Ellin Collins*

☞ Superlatives (World)
(The Largest, Biggest, Smallest, Longest, Highest)

Airport	*Largest*	King Fahd International Airport, near Damman (Saudi Arabia)
Animal	*Tallest*	Giraffe (Average height 6.09 m)
	Largest & Heaviest	Blue Whale (190 tonnes)
	Longest recorded	Boot lace Worm (55 m)
	Fastest	Cheetah (Approximately 100 km/hr)
Bay	*With max. shore line*	Hudson Bay (Canada: 12268 km)
	With maximum area	Bay of Bengal (India: 217 million hc)
Building	*Tallest*	Burj Khalifa in Dubai (818 meter)
Canal	*Big ship (longest)*	Suez Canal (160 km) *Busiest* Kiel Canal (North Sea)
Canyon/Gorge	*Deepest*	Hells Canyon, Snake River (Idaho : 7900 ft)
	Largest	Grand Canyon (Colarado River; USA; 446 km)
Church	*Largest*	Basilica of St. Peter (Vatican City Rome—Area 23000 sq. m.)
City	*Largest in Area*	Jiuquan Gansu, China (Area 1,67,996 Sq km)
Continent	*biggest*	Asia (31,845,872 km^2)
	Smallest	Australia Mainland (Area 76,17,930 km^2)
Country,	*Largest in Population*	China (over 137 crore)
	Largest in Area	Russia (17,098,242 sq. km)
	With largest electorate	India (over 80 crores)
	Smallest independent	State of Vatican City (0.44 km^2)
	With most land frontiers	China (16)
Dam	*Largest (concrete)*	Grand Coulee Dam (1272 m on Columbia River (Washington State, USA)
	Highest	Jinping-I (305 m)
Delta	*Largest*	Sundarban's Ganga-Brahmaputra delta (1,05,000 sq. km)
Desert	*Largest*	Sahara (N. Africa; maximum length 5,150 km EW; maximum width 3,200 km NS)
Diamond	*Largest*	The Cullinan (3106 carats)
Dome	*Largest*	Singapore National Stadium (310 m.)
Epic	*Longest*	Mahabharata
Fish	*Largest fresh water*	Plabeuk (China, Laos and Thailand)
	Most abundant	Bristle mouth
	Most venomous	Stone Fish (Indo-Pacific Waters)
Film	*Most Oscars*	Ben Hur (11 Oscars—1959); Titanic (11 Oscars—1998); The Lord of Rings : The Return of the King (11 Oscars—2003).
Fountain	*Tallest*	King Fahd's Fountain (Jeddah, Saudi Arabia)
Fruit	*Most nutritive*	Avocado (Vitamins A, C, E and Proteins; Central and South America)
	Least nutritive	Cucumber

General Knowledge

Goldmine	*Largest in area*	Grasberg Mines (Fapua, Indonesia)
Gulf	*Largest*	Gulf of Mexico (1,544,000 sq. km)
Hotel	*Tallest*	Gevora, Dubai (356 meter, 75 Floor)
Hotel	*Largest (with most rooms)*	Hotel Rossiya (Moscow; Russia; 12 storey; 3,200 rooms)
Island	*Biggest*	Greenland (now known as Kalaatdlit Nunaat—2,175,600 sq km)
Lake	*Largest*	Caspian Sea (Azerbaijan, Russia, Iran border: 37.18 lakh km^2)
	Deepest	Baikal (Siberia)
	Largest (fresh water)	Superior Lake (USA—Canada border: 82,350 km^2)
Library	*Biggest*	United States Library of Congress (Washington D.C. founded in 1800, contains 101 million items)
	Biggest non-statutory	New York Public Library
Mountain	*Highest peak*	Mt. Everest (8848 m; Nepal)
	Greatest mountain range	Himalaya-Karakoram (96 out of 109 peaks over 7315 m are here)
Museum	*Largest*	American Museum of Natural History, New York
Ocean	*Largest and Deepest*	The Pacific (Area: 166,240,000 km^2; Depth: 10,924 m)
Oscars	*Maximum awards*	Titanic, Benhur (11 each)
Peninsula	*Largest*	Arabia (3.25 million sq. km)
Park	*Largest*	National Park of North-Eastern, Greenland (972000 km^2)
Places	*Rainiest (annual mean)*	Mowsynram near Cherapunji (Meghalaya; India; 11,873 mm)
Planet	*Biggest*	Jupiter (equatorial diameter 142984 km)
	Brightest, hottest and nearest to Earth	Venus
	Nearest to Sun	Mercury
	Most satellites	Jupiter
Plateau	*Highest*	Tibetan Plateau (Central Asia: 4900 m)
Platform	*Longest (rail)*	Gorakhpur (UP)
Port	*Largest*	Port of New York and New Jersey (USA)
Port	*Busiest*	Rotterdam (Netherlands)
Railway Line	*Longest*	Trans-Siberian Railway (Moscow-Nakhodka: 9438 km)
Railway Station	*Largest*	Grand Central Terminal (New York City; 19 hc)
	Highest	Condor (Bolivia; 4786 m)
Religion	*Oldest*	Hinduism
Religion	*Largest*	Christianity
Rivers	*Longest*	(i) Nile (6650 km) (ii) Amazon (6437 km)
Road	*Longest*	Pan American Highway (Alaska—Brasila: 48,000 km)

 General Knowledge

Sea	*Largest*	South China Sea (2,974,600 sq. km)
	Largest (inland)	Mediterranean
Stadium	*Largest*	Strahov Stadium at Prague (Czechoslovakia (240,000 spectators)
Star	*Brightest*	Sirius A (also called Dog Star)
Swimming course	*Longest recognised*	English Channel
Temple	*Largest*	Angkor Vat (Cambodia: 402 acres)
Tower	*Tallest*	Sky Tree, Tokyo, Japan
Train	*Fastest*	Japan's magnetically levitated (magler) train (Speed over 500 km/hr)
Tunnel	*Longest (railway)*	Gotthard Base Rail Tunnel (Switzerland; 57.1 km)
	Largest (road)	Laerdal, Norway (24.51 km)
Wall	*Longest*	Great Wall of China (main length 3460 km; branches length 2860 km)
Waterfall	*Highest*	Salto-Angel (in Venezuela on a branch of river Carrao, 807 m.)
	Largest	Khone Falls (Laos; width 10.8 km)
Zoo	*Largest*	Etosha Reserve (Namibia; area 10 million hc approx.).

☞ Capital & Currencies

Country	Capital	Currency	Country	Capital	Currency
✷ Afghanistan	Kabul	Afghani	✷ Bosnia Herzegovina	Sarajevo	Dinar
✷ Albania	Tirana	Lek			
✷ Algeria	Algiers	Dinar	✷ Bulgaria	Sofia	Lev
✷ Angola	Luanda	New Kwanza	✷ Cambodia	Phnom-Penh	Riel
✷ Argentina	Buenos Aires	Peso	✷ Canada	Ottawa	Dollar
✷ Armenia	Yeravan	Dram	✷ Chile	Santiago	Peso
✷ Australia	Canberra	Dollar	✷ China	Beijing	Yuan
✷ Austria	Vienna	Euro	✷ Colombia	Bogota	Peso
✷ Azerbaijan	Baku	Manat	✷ Congo	Brazzaville	Franc
✷ Bahrain	Manama	Dinar	✷ Croatia	Zagreb	Kuna
✷ Bangladesh	Dhaka	Taka	✷ Cuba	Havana	Peso
✷ Barbados	Bridgetown	Dollar	✷ Cyprus	Nicosia	Pound
✷ Belarus	Minsk	Ruble	✷ Czech Republic	Prague	Koruna
✷ Belgium	Brussels	Euro			
✷ Benin	Porto Novo	Franc	✷ Denmark	Copenhagen	Krone
✷ Bhutan	Thimphu	Ngultrum[1]	✷ Ecuador	Quito	Sucre
✷ Bolivia	La paz	Dollar	✷ Egypt	Cairo	Pound
✷ Botswana	Gaborone	Pula	✷ Estonia	Tallinn	Kroon
✷ Brazil	Brasilia	Real			

1. *Fixed at par with Indian Rupee.*

General Knowledge

Country	Capital	Currency	Country	Capital	Currency
✳ Ethiopia	Addis Ababa	Birr	✳ New Zealand	Wellington	Dollar
✳ Fiji	Suva	Dollar	✳ Nigeria	Abuja	Naira
✳ Finland	Helsinki	Euro	✳ Norway	Oslo	Krone
✳ France	Paris	Euro	✳ Oman	Muscat	Rial
✳ Georgia	Tbilisi	Lari	✳ Pakistan	Islamabad	Rupee
✳ Germany	Berlin	Euro	✳ Panama	Panama City	Balboa
✳ Ghana	Accra	Cedi	✳ Peru	Lima	New Sole
✳ Greece	Athens	Euro	✳ Philippines	Manila	Peso
✳ Guatemala	Guatemala City	Quetzal	✳ Poland	Warsaw	Zloty
			✳ Portugal	Lisbon	Euro
✳ Guyana	George Town	Dollar	✳ Qatar	Doha	Riyal
✳ Hungary	Budapest	Forint	✳ Romania	Bucharest	Leu
✳ Iceland	Reykjavik	Krona	✳ Russia	Moscow	Ruble
✳ India	New Delhi	Rupee	✳ Saudi Arabia	Riyadh	Rial
✳ Indonesia	Jakarta	Rupiah	✳ Senegal	Dakar	Franc
✳ Iran	Teheran	Rial	✳ Slovakia	Bratislava	Koruna (Crown)
✳ Iraq	Baghdad	Dinar			
✳ Ireland	Dublin	Euro	✳ Spain	Madrid	Euro
✳ Israel	Jerusalem	Shekel	✳ Sri Lanka	Colombo	Rupee
✳ Italy	Rome	Euro	✳ Sudan	Khartoum	Dinar
✳ Jamaica	Kingston	Dollar	✳ Suriname	Paramaribo	Guilder
✳ Japan	Tokyo	Yen	✳ Sweden	Stockholm	Krona
✳ Jordan	Amman	Dinar	✳ Switzerland	Berne	Swiss Francs
✳ Kazakhstan	Akmola	Tenge	✳ Syria	Damascus	Pound
✳ Kenya	Nairobi	Shilling	✳ South Africa	Capetown (Legislative)	Rand
✳ Korea (S)	Seoul	Won		Pretoria (Administrative)	
✳ Korea (N)	Pyongyang	Won			
✳ Kyrgyzstan	Bishkek	Som			
✳ Kuwait	Kuwait City	Dinar	✳ Tadzhikistan	Dushanbe	Ruble
✳ Laos	Vientiane	Kip	✳ Taiwan	Taipei	Dollar
✳ Latvia	Riga	Lats	✳ Tanzania	Dodoma	Shilling
✳ Lebanon	Beirut	Pound	✳ Thailand	Bangkok	Baht
✳ Liberia	Monrovia	Dollar	✳ Tunisia	Tunis	Dinar
✳ Libya	Tripoli	Dinar	✳ Turkey	Ankara	Lira
✳ Lithuania	Vilnius	Litas	✳ Turkmania	Ashikabad	Manat
✳ Luxembourg	Luxembourg	Euro	✳ Uganda	Kampala	Shilling
✳ Macedonia	Skopje	Dinar	✳ Ukraine	Kiev	Hyrvnia
✳ Malawi	Lilongwe	Kwacha	✳ United Arab Emirates	Abu Dhabi	Dirham
✳ Malaysia	Kuala Lumpur	Ringgit			
✳ Maldives	Male	Rufiyaa	✳ U.K.	London	Pound Sterling
✳ Mali	Bamako	Franc			
✳ Mauritius	Port Louis	Rupee	✳ U.S.A.	Washington	Dollar
✳ Mexico	Mexico City	Peso	✳ Uruguay	Montevideo	Peso
✳ Moldavia	Chisinau	Leu	✳ Uzbekistan	Tashkent	Som
✳ Mongolia	Ulan Bator	Tugrik	✳ Venezuela	Caracas	Bolivar
✳ Morocco	Rabat	Dirham	✳ Vietnam	Hanoi	Dong
✳ Mozambique	Maputo	Metical	✳ Yemen	Sana'a	Rial
✳ Myanmar	Nay Pyi Taw	Kyat	✳ Zimbabwe	Harare	Dollar
✳ Namibia	Winohoek	Dollar	✳ Congo (Zaire)	Kinshasa	Zaire
✳ Nepal	Kathmandu	Rupee	✳ Zambia	Lusaka	Kwacha
✳ Netherlands	Amsterdam	Euro			

 **General Knowledge**

☞ Geographical Explorations/Discoveries

Place	Explorer/Discoverer	Nationality	Year
America	Christopher Columbus	Italy	1492
Hawaii Islands (Sandwich Islands)	Captain James Cook	England	1778
Newfoundland	John Cabot	England	1497
New Zealand	Abel Janszoon Tasman	Holland	1642
North Pole	Robert Peary	USA	1909
Sea Route to India (via Cape of Good Hope)	Vasco da Gama	Portugal	1498
South Pole	Roald Amundsen	Norway	1911

☞ World Famous Official Documents

* **White Paper:** India
* **Orange Book:** Netherlands
* **Yellow Book:** France
* **Green Book:** Italy and Iran
* **White Book:** Portugal, China and Germany
* **Grey Book:** Japan and Belgium.

☞ Animals (Largest and Biggest)

Fastest animal at short run	Cheetah
Largest existing land animal	Elephant
Largest bird of prey	Condor, length of the bird is 4 ft.
Largest neck (animal)	Giraffe
Largest quadruped of the dog family	Wolf
Largest animal of the cat family	Lion
Largest ape or anthropoid	Goerilla
Largest sea animal (mammal)	Blue whale
Smallest bird	Humming bird
Longest lived creature	Blue whale (500 years)
Most intelligent animal	Chimpanzee
Tallest animal	Giraffe
Largest bird	Ostrich
The bird that never makes its nest	Cuckoo
Largest sea-bird	Albatross
Fastest bird	Swift
The tree that weeps	Laurel tree, in the Canary Islands
The bird that hides itself in sand, when attacked	Ostrich
The wingless bird or flightless bird	Kiwi (New Zealand)
The animal that can shakes off its tail	Whale
The reptile which changes its colour	Chameleon
The tree from which cricket bat is obtained	Willow

☞ National Monuments of Some Famous Countries

Monument	Country	Monument	Country
Great Wall of China	China	Pyramid (Giza)	Egypt
Taj Mahal (Agra)	India	Kinder Disk	Denmark
Emperial Palace (Tokyo)	Japan	Leaning Tower of Pisa	Italy
Opera House (Sydney)	Australia	Statue of Liberty (New York)	USA
Eiffel Tower (Paris)	France	Kremlin (Moscow)	Russia

General Knowledge

☞ The Seven Wonders of the World

Ancient World	Modern World	The 'New' Wonder
✳ The Great Pyramid of Giza	Panama Canal	The Taj Mahal, India
✳ The Temple of Artemis at Ephesus	Channel Tunnel	Chichen Itza, Mexico
✳ The Lighthouse of Alexandria	CN Tower	Machu Picchu, Peru
✳ The Mausoleum at Halicarnassus	Itaipu Dam	Christ Redeemer, Brazil
✳ The Colossus	Empire State Building	Petra, Jordan
✳ The Hanging Gardens of Babylon	Golden Gate Bridge	Colosseum, Italy
✳ The Statue of Zeus of Olympia	Delta Works	The Great Wall, China

☞ Intelligence Agencies of Some Prominent Countries

Country	Intelligence Agency
✳ India	Research & Analysis Wing (RAW), Intelligence Bureau (I.B.), Central Bureau of Investigation (C.B.I.)
✳ Pakistan	Inter Service Intelligence (I.S.I.)
✳ U.S.A.	Central Intelligence Agency, Federal Bureau of Investigation
✳ Britain	Military Intelligence (M.I.)-5 and 6, Special Branch, Ultra, Joint Intelligence Organisation
✳ Israel	Mosad
✳ Egypt	Mukhabarat
✳ Japan	Nicho
✳ Russia	K.G.B. (Komitel Gosudarstvennoy Bezopasnosty) (Committee for State Security)
✳ Canada	Security Intelligence Service
✳ S. Africa	Bureau of State Security
✳ Iran	Sabak
✳ Iraq	Al-Mukhabarat
✳ Australia	Australian Security and Intelligence Organisation
✳ France	S.D.E.C.E.
✳ Spain	C.E.S.I.D.

☞ Important Symbols or Signs

✳ White Flag	Symbol of truce
✳ Red Flag	Revolution; also sign of danger
✳ Black Flag	Symbol of protest
✳ Yellow Flag	Flown on ships or vehicles carrying patients suffering from infectious diseases
✳ Flag flown upside down	Symbol of distress
✳ Flag flown at half mast	Symbol of national mourning
✳ Olive Branch	Symbol of peace
✳ Wheel (Chakra)	Symbol of progress
✳ One skull on two bones crossing each other diagonally	Sign of danger
✳ Pen	Symbol of culture and civilisation
✳ Lotus	Culture and civilisation
✳ Red Cross	Medical aid and hospital
✳ Pigeon or Dove	Symbol of peace
✳ A blindfolded woman holding a balanced scale	Symbol of justice
✳ Black strip on face arm	Sign of mourning or protest

☞ Major Languages of the World and their Speakers

Listing the languages spoken by approximately 1% of humankind (those spoken by more than 60,000,000 people), this table enumerates speakers of each tongue as a primary language.

Language	Speakers (millions)	Language	Speakers (millions)
* Chinese	1,283	* Korean	77
* Spanish	436	* French	76
* English	372	* Telugu	74
* Hindi	260	* Marathi	71
* Arabic	295	* Turkish	71
* Portuguese	218	* Tamil	68
* Bengali	242	* Vietnamese	68
* Russian	153	* Urdu	69
* Japanese	128	* Italian	63
* Javanese	84	* Punjabi (Western)	93
* Lahnda	118	* Malay	60
* German	76	* Persian	61

(Source: The World Almanac-2018)

☞ Famous Newspapers of the World

Newspaper	Place of Publishing	Language	Newspaper	Place of Publishing	Language
* Daily News	New York (America)	*English*	* Daily Mirror	Britain	*English*
* Guardian	London (Britain)	*English*	* Hindu, Hindustan, Times of India,		
* Pravada	Moscow (Russia)	*Russian*	Tribune, Statesman,		
* Al-Ahram	Cairo (Egypt)	*Arabic*	Indian Express, Economic		
* Merdeca	Jakarta (Indonesia)	*Indonesian*	Times	India	*English*
* Times	London (Britain)	*English*	* Hindustan, Nav Bharat Times,		
* People's Daily	Beijing (China)	*Chinese*	Rashtriya Sahara, Dainik Jagaran, Punjab		
* New Statesman	Britain	*English*	Kesari	India	*Hindi*

☞ Important News Agencies of the World

Agency	Country	Agency	Country
PTI, UNI, UNIVARTA	India	Antara	Indonesia
Tanjug	Serbia	Associated Press (AP)	America
Reuters, NAFEN	United Kingdom	Angence France Press (AFP)	France
TASS	Russia		

General Knowledge

☞ Name of Parliaments of Some Countries

Country	Name of Parliament	Country	Name of Parliament
Afghanistan	Shora	Norway	Storting
Argentina	National Congress	Poland	Sejm
Australia	Federal Parliament	Russia	Federal Assembly (Council of the Federation and State Duma
Austria	National Assembly		
Bangladesh	Jatiya Sangsad		
India	Lok Sabha and Rajya Sabha	South Africa	National Assembly and Senate
Bhutan	Tshogdu (National Assembly)	Spain	Cortes Generales
		Sweden	Riksdag
Britain	House of Commons and House of Lords	Switzerland	Federal Assembly (Nationalrat and Standerat)
Canada	House of Commons and Senate	North Korea	Supreme People's Assembly
China	National People Congress	South Korea	National Assembly
Denmark	Folketing	U.S.A.	Congress (Senate and House of Representatives)
Iran	Majlis (Islamic Consultative Assembly)		
Israel	Knesset	Ethiopia	Federal Council and House of Representatives
Japan	Diet		
Myanmar	Pyithu Hluttaw (People's Assembly)	Iceland	Alpingi
		Bulgaria	National Assembly
Nepal	Rashtriya Panchayat	Cuba	National Assembly of People's Power
The Netherlands	States-General		

☞ Largest and Smallest Countries (Top 5)

Largest Country (Area-wise)	Largest Country (Population-wise)	Smallest Country (Area-wise)	Smallest Country (Population-wise)
Russia	China	Vatican City	Vactican City
Canada	India	Monaco	Tuvalu
China	USA	Nauru	Nauru
United States	Indonesia	Tuvalu	Palau
Brazil	Brazil	San Marino	San Marino

☞ Religions of the World

Religion	Member	Percentage	Religion	Member	Percentage
Christianity	2.4 billion	32.9%	Buddhism	521 million	7.0%
Islam	1.7 billion	23.6%	Sikhism	25 million	0.3%
Hinduism	1.0 billion	13.7%			

General Knowledge

☞ **National Emblems of Important Countries**

Country	National Emblem	Country	National Emblem
America	Golden Rod	New Zealand	Kiwi, Fern
Australia	Kangaroo		Southern Cross
Ireland	Shamrock	Norway	Lion
Italy	White Lily	Nepal	Kukri
Israel	Candelabrum	Pakistan	Crescent
Iran	Rose	Poland	Eagle
Canada	White Lily	France	Lily
Great Britain	Rose	Belgium	Lion
Chile	Candor and Huemul	Bangladesh	Water Lily
Germany	Corn Flower	Mongolia	The Soyombo
Japan	Chrysanthemum	Russia	Double headed eagle
Zimbabwe	Zimbabwe Bird	Lebanon	Cedar Tree
Denmark	Beach	Sudan	Secretary Bird
Turkey	Crescent and Star	Syria	Eagle
The Netherlands	Lion	India	Lioned Capital

☞ **First in India**

✴ The first Indian to get the Nobel Prize for Literature	*Rabindra Nath Tagore*
✴ The first Indian to get the Nobel Prize for Physics	*C.V. Raman*
✴ The first Indian to get the Nobel Prize for Peace	*Mother Teresa*
✴ The first Indian to get the Nobel Prize for Economics	*Amartya Sen*
✴ The first Indian to get Special Oscar award (1992)	*Satyajit Ray*
✴ The first and the last Indian Governor-General of free India	*C. Rajagopalachari*
✴ The first woman to become the Governor of a State	*Smt. Sarojini Naidu*
✴ The first Indian Chief of the Army Staff*	*General K.M. Cariappa*
✴ The first ever woman to become the Chief Minister of a State	*Smt. Sucheta Kripalani*
✴ The first Indian woman President of UN General Assembly	*Smt. Vijaylakshmi Pandit*
✴ The first Indian to become the President of Inter. Court of Justice	*Dr. Nagendra Singh*
✴ The first Indian woman to swim across the English Channel	*Ms. Aarti Saha*
✴ The first Indian girl to become Miss Universe	*Miss Sushmita Sen*
✴ The first Indian girl to become Miss World	*Rita Faria*
✴ The first Indian to swim across the English Channel	*Mihir Sen*
✴ The first Field Marshal	*S.H.F.J. Manekshaw*
✴ The first Indian recipient of Victoria Cross	*Khudadad Khan*
✴ The first Indian to conquer Mt. Everest	*Sherpa Tenzing (May 29, 1953)*
✴ The first Indian Cosmonaut (man)	*Rakesh Sharma (April 3, 1984)*
✴ The first Indian Cosmonaut (woman)	*Kalpana Chawla (Nov. 19, 1997)*
✴ The first woman to climb Mt. Everest	*Miss Bachendri Pal (May 23, 1984)*
✴ The first ICS	*Satyendranath Tagore*

General Knowledge

✳ The first to address the UN General Assembly in Hindi	Atal Bihari Vajpai
✳ The first Newspaper	Bengal Gazette (Jan 27, 1780)
✳ The first Postage Stamp issued	In 1852
✳ The first Telegraph line laid	In 1851 (Calcutta-Diamond Harbour)
✳ The first Railways run	April 16, 1853 (Bombay-Thane)
✳ The first Electric Train run	1925 (Bombay-Kurla)
✳ The first Atomic Power Station	Tarapore (Maharashtra)
✳ The first passenger-cum-cargo ship made in India	Harshavardhan
✳ The first Satellite	Aryabhatta (1975)
✳ The first President of the Indian National Congress	W.C. Banerjee
✳ The first President of Indian Republic	Dr. Rajendra Prasad
✳ The first woman judge of the Supreme Court	Ms Fatima Bibi
✳ The first to climb Everest without oxygen	Phu Dorjee (1987)
✳ The first film (movie)	Raja Harishchandra
✳ The first film (talkie)	Alam Ara
✳ The first Metro Railway	Calcutta Metro Railway
✳ The first Test-tube baby, scientifically documented	Born on August 6, 1986 at K.E.M. Hospital, Bombay
✳ The first TV Centre	At Delhi
✳ The first Indian to get an Oscar	Bhanu Athaiya
✳ The first woman pilot in IAF	Ms Harita Kaur Deol
✳ The first woman to get Olympic Medal	Karnam Malleswari
✳ The first woman Foreign Secretary	Chokila Iyer

☞ Superlatives (India)

Highest, Biggest, Largest and Longest in India

✳ Award for Gallantry, highest	Param Vir Chakra
✳ Award, highest civilian	Bharat Ratna
✳ Bank, with largest number of branches	State Bank of India
✳ Road Bridge, Longest	Bhupen Hazarika Setu Across Lohit River, Assam (9.15 km.)
✳ Cattle Fair, Largest	Sonepur (Bihar)
✳ City, Most Populous	Mumbai metropolis
✳ Corridor, Longest	Rameshwaram Temple corridor (4,000 ft.)
✳ Desert, Largest	Thar (Rajasthan)
✳ Dam, Longest	Hirakud Dam (Odisha)
✳ Delta, Largest	Sunderban's Delta
✳ Dome, Largest	Gol Gumbaj (Bijapur)
✳ Dam, Highest	Tehri Dam (855 ft.)
✳ Gateway, Highest	Buland Darwaja at Fatehpur Sikri (176 ft.)
✳ Lake, Largest (Fresh Water)	Wular Lake (Kashmir)
✳ Literacy, Highest	Kerala
✳ Museum, Largest	Indian Museum (Kolkata)

✳ Mosque, Biggest	*Jama Masjid (Delhi)*
✳ Peak, Highest*	*K-2 (Pak-Occupied Kashmir)*
✳ Platform, Longest	*At Gorakhpur, NE Railway (1335.4 mtrs)*
✳ Railway Bridge, longest (on river)	*Nehru Setu (river Sone: 10,044 ft.)*
✳ Railway route, longest	*Passenger train-Dibrugarh to Kanyakumari (4,286 km).*
✳ River, Longest**	*The Ganges (2525 Km)*
✳ Rainfall, Highest (annual mean)	*Mowsynram near Cherrapunji (1178 cm)*
✳ Road Longest	*Grand Trunk Road (1,500 miles)*
✳ State, with maximum forest cover	*Madhya Pradesh*
✳ State, with maximum density of population	*Bihar*
✳ Telescope, Largest in Asia	*Vainu Bappu Telescope (at Kavalur: Chennai) 2.34m*
✳ Tunnel, Longest (Road)	*Chenani-Nashri Tunnel (J&K 9.28 kms)*
✳ Tunnel, Longest (Railway)	*Between Banihal and Qazigund stations in J&K (11.21 km)*
✳ Tower, Highest	*Qutub Minar (Delhi 72.5 m.)*
✳ Waterfall, Highest	*Gersoppa Waterfall (Karnataka: 960 ft.)*
✳ Zoo, Largest	*Zoological Gardens (Kolkata)*

* *Highest peak in the world is Mount Everest, which is in Nepal. K-2 is the second highest peak in the world. It is 8,611 metres high.*
** *Indus and Brahmaputra (each 2900 km). Both of them, however, cover a long distance outside India.*

☞ Table of Precedence

1. President

2. Vice-President

3. Prime Minister

4. Governors of States within their respective states

5. Former Presidents

5A. Deputy Prime Minister

6. Chief Justice of India, Speaker of Lok Sabha

7. Cabinet Ministers of the Union, Chief Ministers of States within their respective States, Deputy Chairman NITI Aayog, Former Prime Ministers.

   Leaders of opposition in Rajya Sabha and Lok Sabha

7A. Holders of the Bharat Ratna Decoration

8. Ambassadors Extraordinary and Plenipotentiary and High Commissioners of Commonwealth Countries accredited to India, Chief Ministers of States outside their respective States, Governors of States outside their respective states.

9. Judges of the Supreme Court

9A. Chairperson Union Public Service Commission, Chief Election Commissioner, Comptroller & Auditor-General of India.

10. Deputy Chairman Rajya Sabha, Deputy Chief Minister of States, Deputy Speaker Lok Sabha, Members of the NITI Aayog, Minister of State of the Union and Other Minister in the Ministry of Defence.

General Knowledge

☞ Books and Authors

FOREIGN

Book	Author
As You Like It	William Shakespeare
A Tale of Two Cities	Charles Dickens
Ben Hur	Lewis Wallace
Das Kapital	Karl Marx
David Copperfield	Charles Dickens
Hamlet	William Shakespeare
Iliad	Homer
Inferno	A. Dante
In Memoriam	Lord Tennyson
Ivanhoe	Walter Scott
Julius Caesar	William Shakespeare
Lady Chatterley's Lover	D.H. Lawrence
Lajja	Taslima Nasreen
Les Miserable	Victor Hugo
Leviathan	Thomas Hobbes
Lolita	V. Nobokov
Lycidas	John Milton
Mein Kampf	Adolf Hitler
Moor's Last Sigh	Salman Rushdie
Mother	Maxim Gorky
Mother India	Katherine Mayo
Nana	Emile Zola
Odyssey	Homer
Origin of Species	Charles Darwin
Othello	William Shakespeare
Paradise Lost	John Milton
Paradise Regained	John Milton
Path to Power	Margaret Thatcher
Pickwick Papers	Charles Dickens
Razor's Edge	Somerset Maugham
Republic	Plato
The Tempest	William Shakespeare
Time Machine	H.G. Wells
Tom Sawyer	Mark Twain
Treasure Island	R.L. Stevenson
Twelfth Night	William Shakespeare
Unto This Last	John Ruskin
Utopia	Thomas More
Wealth of Nations	Adam Smith
Wonder that was India	A.L. Basham

INDIAN

Book	Author
Ain-i-Akbari	Abul Fazal
Anand Math	Bankim Chandra Chatterjee
Arthashastra	Kautilya
A Suitable Boy	Vikram Seth
Bhagwat Gita	Ved Vyas
Chidambara	Sumitranandan Pant
Devdas	Sarat Chandra Chatterjee
Discovery of India	Jawaharlal Nehru
Ganadevata	Tarashankar Bandopadhyaya
Geet Govind	Jaya Dev
Geetanjali	R. N. Tagore
Glimpses of World History	Jawaharlal Nehru
Godaan	Prem Chand
Gul-e-Nagma	Firaq Gorakhpuri
Harsh Charita	Bana Bhatta
Idols	Sunil Gavaskar
India Divided	Dr. Rajendra Prasad
The Judgement	Kuldip Nayyar
Kadambari	Bana Bhatta
Kagaz Te Kanwas	Amrita Pritam
Kamayani	Jai Shankar Prasad
Kitni Nawon Mein Kitni Bar	S. H. Vatsyayan
Kumar Sambhav	Kalidas
Mahabharata	Ved Vyas
Malgudi Days	R.K. Narayan
Meghdoot	Kalidas
Mritunjaya	B.K. Bhattacharya
Mudrarakshasa	Vishakhadatta
Prison Diary	Jaya Prakash Narayan
Raghuvansha	Kalidas
Rajtarangini	Kalhana
Ramayana	Balmiki
Ramcharit Manas	Tulsidas
Rukh Te Rishi	Harbhajan Singh
Satyarth Prakash	Swami Dayanand
Sur Sagar	Surdas
The Guide	R.K. Narayan

 General Knowledge

☞ **Important Dates and Days of the Year**

★ JANUARY

5-11 Road Safety Week
12 National Youth Day
15 Army Day
15-21 Pin Code Week
23 National Day of Patriotism
26 Republic Day
30 Martyr's Day

★ FEBRUARY

1-14 Oil Conservation Fortnight
14 Valentine's Day

★ MARCH

4 National Safety Day
8 International Women's Day
15 Consumers' Day
21 World Forest Day
22 World Day for Water
24 World Meteorological Day
1-7 Preservation of Blindness Week

★ APRIL

7 World Health Day
7-13 Handloom Week
14-20 Fire Service Week
18 World Heritage Day
22 World Earth Day

★ MAY

1 May Day
5 National Labour Day
8 World Red Cross Day
11 National Technology Day
15 International Day of the Family
17 World Telecommunication Day
24 Commonwealth Day
31 World No-Tobacco Day

★ JUNE

5 World Environment Day
21 International Day of Yoga
26 International Day against Drug Abuse and Illicit Trafficking

★ JULY

11 World Population Day

★ AUGUST

1-7 World Breast feeding Week
10 Sanskrit Divas
15 Independence Day
20 Sadbhavana Divas

★ SEPTEMBER

1-7 National Nutrition Week
5 Teachers' Day
8 International Literary Day
14 Hindi Diwas
23 World Deaf Day
27 World Tourism Day

★ OCTOBER

2 ★ Gandhi Jayanti
★ International Day of Non Violence
★ Anti-Leprosy Day
4 World Animal Day
6 World Habitat Day *(Ist Monday)*
8 Indian Air Force Day
14 World Standard Day
15 International Day of Rural Women
16 World Food Day
24 United Nations Day
27 Infantry Day
28 World Thrift Day
31 Anti-Terrorism Day

★ NOVEMBER

2 All Saints Day
14 Children's Day
15-21 National Cooperative Week
19-25 Quami Ekta Week
20 Child Rights Day
26 Constitution Day

★ DECEMBER

1 World AIDS Day
3 World Day for the Disabled
4 Naval Day
7 Flag Day
8 SMRC Day
10 Human Rights Day
14 National Energy Conservation Day

General Knowledge

ABBREVIATIONS

A

ABC	Atomic, Biological and Chemical (Warfare)
ABM	Anti-Ballistic Missile
ACC	Auxiliary Cadet Corpse
ACD	Asian Co-operation Dialogue
AD	Anno Domini (in the year of Our Lord)
ADB	Asian Development Bank
AEC	Atomic Energy Commission
AFSPA	Armed Forces Special Power Act
AICC	All India Congress Committee
AIDS	Acquired Immune Deficiency Syndrome
AIIMS	All India Institute of Medical Sciences
AITUC	All India Trade Union Congress
AMP	Auto Mission Plan
ANC	African National Congress
APPLE	Ariane Passenger Payload Experiment
ARC	Administrative Reforms Commission
ASEAN	Association for South East Asian Nations
ASI	Archaeological Survey of India
ASLV	Augmented Satellite Launch Vehicle
ATM	Automated Teller Machine

B

BA	Bachelor of Arts, British Academy
BARC	Bhabha Atomic Research Centre
BBC	British Broadcasting Corporation
BC	Before Christ
BCG	Bacillus Calmette Guerim (Anti-TB Vaccine)
BCCI	Board of Control for Cricket in India
BHEL	Bharat Heavy Electricals Limited
BRAI	Broadcast Regulatory Authority of India
BSF	Border Security Force
BSNL	Bharat Sanchar Nigam Limited

C

CA	Chartered Accountant
CAC	Consumer Access Codes
CBI	Central Bureau of Investigation
CBSE	Central Board of Secondary Education
CBDT	Central Board of Direct Taxes
CDMA	Code Division Multiple Axis
CDS	Compulsory Deposit Scheme
CISF	Central Industrial Security Force
CID	Criminal Investigation Department
COCA	Control of Organised Crime Act
CPCB	Central Pollution Control Board
CRPF	Central Reserve Police Force
CRR	Cash Reserve Ratio
CSIR	Council of Scientific & Industrial Research
CVR	Cockpit Voice Recorder
CVC	Central Vigilance Commission

D

DDT	Dichloro-Diphenyl Trichloroethane (disinfectant)
DGCA	Director General of Civil Aviation
DIG	Deputy Inspector General
DNA	Deoxy-ribo Nucleic Acid
DOD	Department of Ocean Development
DPSA	Deep Penetration Strike Aircraft
DRDO	Defence Research Development Organisation
DSIDC	Defence Scientific Information and Documentation

E

ECG	Electro Cardiogram
ECO	Economic Cooperation Organisation
ECOSOC	Economic and Social Council (UN)
EDUSAT	Education Sattelite
EEC	European Economic Commission
EMS	European Monetary System
ESI	Employees State Insurance
ESRO	European Space Research Organisation

F

FAO	Food and Agriculture Organisation
FBI	Federal Bureau of Investigation
FERA	Foreign Exchange Regulation Act
FERB	Foreign Exchange Regulatory Board
FICCI	Federation of Indian Chambers of Commerce and Industry

G

GAIL	Gas Authority of India Limited
GATT	General Agreement on Tariffs and Trade
GMT	Greenwich Mean Time
GNP	Gross National Product
GPRS	General Packet Radio Service
GSLV	Geo-Satellite Launch Vehicle
GSM	Global System for Mobile Communications
GST	Goods and Services Tax

H

HAL	Hindustan Aeronautics Limited
HDC	Hill Development Council
HEC	Heavy Engineering Corporation
HUDCO	Housing and Urban Development Corporation

I

IAA	International Airports Authority
IA	Indian Airlines
IAF	Indian Air Force
IARI	Indian Agricultural Research Institute
IAS	Indian Administrative Service
IBM	International Business Machines
ICC	International Cricket Council
ICICI	Industrial Credit and Investment Corporation of India
ICMR	Indian Council of Medical Research
ICS	Indian Civil Service
ICWA	Indian Council of World Affairs
IDA	International Development Agency
IDBI	Industrial Development Bank of India
IFFI	International Film Festival of India
IFS	Indian Foreign Service
IGNOU	Indira Gandhi National Open University
IIT	Indian Institute of Technology

I

ILO	International Labour Organisation
INTERPOL	International Police Organisation
IOC	Indian Oil Corporation
IPL	Indian Premier League
ISD	International Subscriber Dialling
ISRO	Indian Space Research Organisation
ISI	Indian Standard Institution
IST	Indian Standard Time
ITI	Indian Telephone Industries; Industrial Training Institute
ITO	International Trade Organisation

J

JCO	Junior Commissioned Officer
JKLF	Jammu and Kashmir Liberation Front
JMM	Jharkhand Mukti Morcha
JPC	Joint Parliamentary Committee

K

KMT	Kuomintang (Nationalist Party of Taiwan)
KANU	Kenya African National Union

L

LASER	Light Amplification by Stimulated Emission of Radiation
LCA	Light Combat Aircraft
LIC	Life Insurance Corporation
LPG	Liquified Petroleum Gas

M

MBA	Master of Business Administration
MBBS	Bachelor of Medicine and Bachelor of Surgery
MCC	Maoits Communist Centre
MI	Military Intelligence
MLA	Member of Legislative Assembly
MNC	Multi-National Company
MODVAT	Modified Value Added Tax

N

NABARD	National Bank for Agriculture and Rural Development
NASA	National Aeronautics and Space Administration (USA)
NASDAQ	National Association of Securities Dealers Automated Quotation
NATO	North Atlantic Treaty Organisation

General Knowledge

NCC	National Cadet Corpse
NCERT	National Council of Educational Research and Training
NCST	National Committee of Science and Technology
NDA	National Defence Academy
NDRI	National Dairy Research Institute
NHAI	National Highway Authority of India
NHRC	National Human Rights Commission
NMD	National Missile Defence

O

OAPEC	Organisation of Arab Petroleum Exporting Countries
OCS	Overseas Communication Service
OPEC	Organisation of Petroleum Exporting Countries

P

PA	Personal Assistant, Press Association
PAN	Permanent Account Number
PERDA	Pension Fund Regulatory and Development Authority
POTA	Prevention of Terrorism Act
PWG	Peoples War Group

Q

QMG	Quarter Master General
QMT	Quantitative Management Technique

R

RADAR	Radio Detecting and Ranging
RAF	Rapid Action Force
RAW	Research & Analysis Wing
RBI	Reserve Bank of India
RCC	Reinforced Cement Concrete

S

SAARC	South Asian Association for Regional Cooperation
SAHR	South Asian for Human Rights
SAFTA	South Asian Free Trade Agreement
SALT	Strategic Arms Limitations Talks
SCRA	Special Class Railway Apprentices
SEBI	Securities and Exchange Board of India
SEZ	Special Economic Zone
SEATO	South-East Asia Treaty Organisation
SHO	Station House Officer
SIM	Subscriber Identification Module

T

TAR	Trans Asian Railways
TISCO	Tata Iron and Steel Company
TRAI	Telecom Regulatory Authority of India
TRYSEM	Training of Rural Youth for Self Employment

U

UTI	Unit Trust of India
UNESCO	United Nations Educational Scientific and Cultural Organisation
UNFPA	United Nations Fund for Population Activities
UNHCR	United Nations High Commission for Refugees
UNICEF	United Nations International Children's Emergency Fund
UNFCC	United Nations Framework Convention on Climate Change.

V

VAT	Value Added Tax
VC	Vice-Chancellor
VHP	Vishwa Hindu Parishad
VIP	Very Important Person
VPP	Value Payable Post
VRS	Voluntary Retirement Scheme

W

WEF	World Environment Forum
wef	with effect from
WHO	World Health Organisation
WFP	World Food Programme
WWF	World Wild-Life Fund
WTO	World Trade Organisation
WWW	World Wide Wave

Z

ZETA	Zero Energy Thermal-nuclear Assembly or Apparatus
ZIP	Zonal Improvement Plan
ZPG	Zero Population Growth

INDIAN DEFENCE

- The Supreme Command of the Armed Forces is vested in the hands of the President of the Country.
- The responsibility for national defence, however, rests with the Cabinet. All important questions having a bearing on defence are decided by the Cabinet Committee on Political Affairs, which is presided over by the Prime Minister.
- The Defence Minister is responsible to Parliament for all matters concerning the Defence Services.
- All the administrative and operational control of Armed Forces are exercised by the Ministry of Defence. The three services—Army, Navy and Air Force function through their respective service headquarters headed by the chief of Staff.

☞ Indian Army Commands

Command	HQ Location	Command	HQ Location
Eastern Command	Kolkata	Western Command	Chandigarh
Northern Command	Udhampur	Southern Command	Pune
Central Command	Lucknow	Training Command	Shimla
South-Western Command	Jaipur		

☞ Indian Air Force Commands

Command	HQ Location	Command	HQ Location
Western Air Command	New Delhi	Sout-Western Air Command	Gandhinagar
Central Air Command	Allahabad	Eastern Air Command	Shillong
Southern Air Command	Thiruvananthapuram	Training Command	Bengaluru

☞ Indian Navy Commands

Command	HQ Location	Command	HQ Location
Eastern Naval Command	Vishakhapatnam	Western Naval Command	Mumbai
Southern Naval Command	Cochin		

Army

Navy

Air Force

General Knowledge 

☞ Commissioned Ranks in Defence Services

Army	Navy	Air Force
General	Admiral	Air Chief Marshal
Lieutenant-General	Vice-Admiral	Air Marshal
Major-General	Rear-Admiral	Air Vice-Marshal
Brigadier	Commodor	Air Commodor
Colonel	Captain	Group Captain
Lieutenant-Colonel	Commander	Wing Commander
Major	Lt.Commander	Squadron Leader
Captain	Lieutenant	Flight Lieutenant
Lieutenant	Sub-Lieutenant	Flying Officer

☞ Internal Security Organisations of India

S.No.	Name of Organisation	Year of Creation	Headquarters
1.	Assam Rifles (A.R.)	1835	Shillong
2.	Central Reserve Police Force (CRPF)	1939	New Delhi
3.	Territorial Army	1948	In different States
4.	Indo-Tibetan Border Police	1962	New Delhi
5.	Home Guard	1962	In different States
6.	Coast Guard	1978	New Delhi
7.	Border Security Force (B.S.F.)	1965	New Delhi
8.	Central Industrial Security Force (CISF)	1969	New Delhi
9.	National Security Guard	1984	New Delhi
10.	Police	—	In different States

☞ Commander-in-Chiefs of India

1.	General Roy Bucher	Jan. 1, 1948 — Jan. 14, 1949
2.	General K. M. Kariappa	Jan. 15, 1949 — Jan. 14, 1953
3.	General Maharaj Rajendra Sinhji	Jan. 15, 1953 — March 31, 1955
4.	First Marshal of the Indian Air Force	Arjan Singh

☞ First Chiefs of Staff of Indian Forces

1.	General Maharaj Rajendra Sinhji (Army Staff)	April 1, 1955 — May 14, 1955
2.	Vice Admiral R D. Katari (Naval Staff)	April 22, 1958 — June 4, 1962
3.	Air Marshal Sri Thomas Elmherst (Air Staff)	Aug. 15, 1947 — Feb. 21, 1950

☞ Defence Production Units

1.	Bharat Dynamics Ltd.	Hyderabad
2.	Praga Tools	Hyderabad
3.	Mishra Dhatu Nigam	Hyderabad
4.	Bharat Electronics Ltd.	Bangaluru
5.	Bharat Earthmovers Ltd.	Bangaluru
6.	Heavy Vehicles Ltd.	Avadi, Chennai
7.	Garden Reach Ship Builders and Engineers Ltd.	Kolkata
8.	Mazagaon Dock	Mumbai
9.	Goa Shipyard	Marmugao
10.	Hindustan Shipyard Ltd.	Vishakhapatnam
11.	Hindustan Aeronautics Ltd.	Bangalore, Hyderabad, Nasik, Koraput, Kanpur, Lucknow

☞ Army Institutes

1. Sainik Schools upto +2 Level	18 places in India
2. Rashtriya Indian Military College (prepare for entrance to N.D.A.)	Dehradun
3. National Defence Academy (three services)	Khadakwasla, Pune
4. Indian Military Academy (Army)	Dehradun
5. Officers Training Academy (3 services) Short Courses	Chennai
6. National Defence College	New Delhi
7. The College of Combat	Mhow
8. The College of Military Engineering	Kirkee
9. Military College of Telecommunication Engineering	Mhow
10. The Armoured Corps Centre and School	Ahmed Nagar
11. The School Artillery	Deolali
12. The Infantry School	Mhow and Belgaum
13. College of Material Management	Jabalpur

☞ Air Force Institutions

✶ Air Force Academy	Hyderabad	✶ The College of Air Warfare	Secunderabad
✶ Helicopter Training School	Hakimpet	✶ Air Force Administrative College	Coimbatore
✶ Flying Instructors School	Tambaram, Chennai	✶ Air Force Technical College	Jalahalli

☞ Missile and Other Weapons

Name	Class	Range	Name	Class	Range
✶ Agni I	SRBM	850 km	✶ Brahmos	Supersonic Cruise Missile	290 km
✶ Agni II	MRBM	2500 km			
✶ Agni III	IRBM	3500 km-5500 km			
✶ Agni IV *or* Agni II Prime	IRBM	4000 km	✶ Brahmos 2	Hypersonic Cruise Missile	290 km
✶ Agni V	ICBM	5000 km-6000 km	✶ Prithvi I	SRBM	150 km
✶ Agni VI	ICBM	8000 km-10000 km	✶ Prithvi III	SRBM	350 km
✶ Agni 3SL	ICBM	5200 km-11600 km	✶ Sagarika	SLBM	700 km-2200 km
✶ Dhanush	SRBM	350 km	✶ Shaurya	TBM	700 km-2200 km
✶ Nirbhay	Subsonic Cruise Missile	1000 km	✶ Astra	Air to Air Missile	80 km-100 km

General Knowledge

UNITED NATIONS ORGANISATION (UNO)

- The United Nations (UN) is an association of states which have pledged themselves to maintain international peace and security and cooperate in solving international political, economic, social cultural and humanitariam problems towards achieving this end.
- Trygve Lie of Norway (1946-52) was the first Secretary-General of the UN.
- Antonio Guterres of Portugal is the present Secretary-General of the UN.
- *Origin:* UN Charter was signed by 50 members on June 26, 1945. Poland signed the charter later to become one of the original 51 member-states. It officially came into existence on October 24, 1945.
- *UN Charter:* The Charter is the Constitution of the UNO and contains its aims and objectives and rules and regulations for its functioning.
- *Aims and Objectives:* They are security, welfare and human rights.
- *Headquarters:* New York.
- *Flag:* The flag is light blue in colour, and emblazoned in white, in its centre is the UN symbol—a polar map of world embraced by twin olive branches open at the top.
- *Official Languages:* The official languages of the UN are: English, French, Chinese, Russian, Arabic and Spanish. However, working languages are English and French only.
- *Present Membership:* At present 193 countries are members of the UNO. South Sudan is the latest entrant to this world organisation.
- *Main Organs of the UNO:* There are six main organs:

1. General Assembly
2. Security Council
3. Economic and Social Council
4. Trusteeship Council
5. International Court of Justice, and
6. Secretariat.

1. *General Assembly:* It consists of representative of all members of the UN. Each member country has only one vote. It meets once a year and passes UN Budget. It is the main place for discussions and policy making in the UN.

2. *Security Council:* It is the Executive body of the UN and is mainly responsible for maintaining international peace and security. It has 15 members, 5 of which (USA, UK, France, Russia and China) are permanent members. The 10 non-permanent members are elected by General Assembly for two-year term and are not eligible for immediate re-election.

3. *Economic and Social Council:* It has 54 members elected by General Assembly.

4. *Trusteeship Council:* It looks after interest of the people in areas not yet independent and leads them towards self-government.

5. *International Court of Justice:* It has 15 judges, no two of whom may be nationals of the same state. They are elected by General Assembly and Security Council for a term of 9 years. The Court elects its President and Vice-President for a 3-year term.

6. *Secretariat:* It is the Secretariat of the UN and is headed by the Secretary General.

☞ **Some Important UN Agencies**

UN Agencies	Headquarters	Year of Establishment
✳ United Nations Organisations (U.N.O.)	New York	1945
✳ International Monetary Fund (I.M.F.)	Washington	1945
✳ World Health Organisation (W.H.O.)	Geneva	1948
✳ Food & Agricultural Organisation (FAO)	Rome	1943
✳ International Labour Organisation (ILO)	Geneva	1919
✳ UNESCO	Paris	1946
✳ Universal Postal Union (UPU)	Berne	1874
✳ UNIDO	Vienna	1967
✳ International Atomic Energy Agency (IAEA)	Vienna	1957
✳ United Nations Development Programme (UNDP)	New York	1965
✳ UNICEF	New York	1946
✳ International Maritime Organisation (IMO)	London	1948
✳ World Meteorological Organisation (WMO)	Geneva	1951
✳ International Telecommunication Union (ITU)	Geneva	1947
✳ World Trade Organisation (WTO)	Geneva	1995
✳ International Development Association (IDA)	Washington D.C.	1960
✳ World Intellectual Property Organisation (WIPO)	Geneva	1967

☞ **Famous International Organisations**

International Organisations	Headquarters	Year of Establishment
✳ International Court of Justice	The Hague	—
✳ International Civil Aviation Organisation (ICAO)	Montreal	1947
✳ International Finance Corporation (IFC)	Washington	1956
✳ Arab League	Tunis	1945
✳ Commonwealth of Nations	London	1931
✳ International Bank for Reconstruction and Development (IBRD)	Washington D.C.	1946
✳ Organisation of Islamic Cooperation (OIC)	Mecca (Saudi Arabia)	1971
✳ European Economic Community (EEC)	Geneva	1957
✳ Red Cross	Geneva	1863
✳ Interpol	Lyons	1923
✳ Asian Development Bank (ADB)	Manila	1966
✳ North Atlantic Treaty Organisation (NATO)	Brussels	1949
✳ Association of South East Asian Nations (ASEAN)	Jakarta	1967
✳ South Asian Association for Regional Cooperation (SAARC)	Kathmandu	1985
✳ Asia-Pacific Economic Cooperation (APEC)	–	1989
✳ Organisation for Economic Cooperation and Development (OECD)	Paris	1961
✳ Organisation of Petroleum Exporting Countries (OPEC)	Vienna	1960
✳ Common Wealth of Independent States (CIS)	Belarus	1991
✳ International Olympic Committee (IOC)	Switzerland	1894
✳ European Union (EU)	Brussels	1965
✳ Amnesty International (AI)	London	1961
✳ Shanghai Cooperation Organisation (SCO)	—	2002

General Knowledge

AWARDS *and* HONOURS

NATIONAL AWARDS

BHARAT RATANA

- Bharat Ratna is India's highest Civilian Award. It was first awarded in 1954.
- The actual award is designed in the shape of a *peepal* leaf with Bharat Ratna inscribed in Devanagri script in the Sun Figure.
- This is India's highest civilian award. It is given for exceptional work on art, literature, science and recognition of public service of the highest order.
- The emblem, the Sun and the rim are of platinum. The inscriptions are in burnished bronze.
- Government servants are not eligible for it. The table shows the recipients of the award:

☞ Bharat Ratna Award Winners:

#	Name	Year	#	Name	Year	#	Name	Year
1.	Dr. S. Radhakrishnan	1954	17.	K. Kamraj	1976	33.	M.S. Subbalakshmi	1998
2.	C. Rajagopalachari	1954	18.	Mother Teresa	1980	34.	C. Subramaniam	1998
3.	Dr. C.V. Raman	1954	19.	Acharya Vinoba Bhave	1983	35.	Jaya Prakash Narayan	1999
4.	Dr. Bhagwan Das	1955	20.	Khan Abdul Ghaffar Khan	1987	36.	Prof. Amartya Sen	1999
5.	Dr. M. Visvesvaraya	1955	21.	M.G. Ramachandran	1988	37.	Pt. Ravi Shankar	1999
6.	Jawahar Lal Nehru	1955	22.	Dr. B.R. Ambedkar	1990	38.	Gopinath Bardoloi	1999
7.	Govind Ballabh Pant	1957	23.	Dr. Nelson R. Mandela	1990	39.	Lata Mangeshkar	2001
8.	Dr. D.K. Karve	1958	24.	Rajiv Gandhi	1991	40.	Bismillah Khan	2001
9.	Dr. Bidhan Chandra Roy	1961	25.	Sardar Vallabhbhai Patel	1991	41.	Bhimsen Joshi	2009
10.	Purushottam Das Tandon	1961	26.	Morarji R. Desai	1991	42.	C.N.R. Rao	2014
11.	Dr. Rajendra Prasad	1962	27.	Maulana Abul Kalam Azad	1992	43.	Sachin Tendulkar	2014
12.	Dr. Zakir Hussain	1963	28.	Jehangir Ratanji Dadabhai Tata	1992	44.	Madan Mohan Malaviya	2015
13.	Dr. Pandurang Vaman Kane	1963	29.	Satyajit Roy	1992	45.	Atal Bihari Vajpayee	2015
14.	Lal Bahadur Shastri	1966	30.	Shri Gulzari Lal Nanda	1997	46.	Nanaji Deshmukh	2019
15.	Indira Gandhi	1971	31.	Mrs. Aruna Asaf Ali	1997	47.	Bhupen Hazarika	2019
16.	V.V. Giri	1975	32.	Dr. A.P.J. Abdul Kalam	1997	48.	Pranab Mukherjee	2019

REPUBLIC DAY AWARDS

Padma Awards

They fall in line after the Bharat Ratna. They are also discontinued in 1977 along with the Bharat Ratna and award was started again in 1980.

There are three Padma Awards:

- *Padma Vibhushan:* This award is given for exceptional and distinguished service in any field, including service rendered by Govt. servants.
- *Padma Bhushan:* This award is given for distinguished service of a high order in any field, including service rendered by Govt. servants.
- *Padma Shri:* This award is given for distinguished service in any field, including service rendered by Government servants.

Gallantry Awards

- *Param Vir Chakra:* The highest award for bravery or some daring and pre-eminent act of valour or self-sacrifice in the presence of the enemy, whether on land, at sea or in the air.
- *Mahavir Chakra:* It is the second highest decoration and is awarded for acts of conspicuous gallantry in the presence of the enemy, whether on land, at sea or in the air.

- *Vir Chakra:* It is the third in order of awards given for acts of gallantry in the presence of enemy, whether on land, at sea or in the air.
- *Ashok Chakra:* This medal is awarded for the most conspicuous bravery or some daring or pre-eminent act of valour or self-sacrifice on land, at sea or in the air but not in the presence of enemy.
- *Vishishta Sewa Medal:* It is awarded to personnel of all the three Services in class I, II and III in recognition of distinguished service of the "most exceptional" and "exceptional" and a "high" order respectively.
- *Jeewan Raksha Padak:* Awarded for meritorious acts or a series of acts of a human nature displayed in saving life from drowning, fire and rescue operations in mines etc.

OTHER NATIONAL AWARDS

NATIONAL SPORTS AWARDS 2018

The President of India, Ram Nath Kovind at a specially organized function at the Rashtrapati Bhawan on September 25, 2018 presented the coveted National sports awards, which are given every year to recognize and reward excellence in sports. Apart from a medal and a citation, Rajiv Gandhi Khel Ratna Awardee received a cash prize of ₹ 7.5 lakh. Arjuna, Dronacharya and Dhyan Chand Awardees received statuettes, certificates and cash prize of ₹ 5 lakh each. The award includes:

- *Rajiv Gandhi Khel Ratna 2018:* Mirabai Chanu (Weightlifting), Virat Kohli (Cricket).

- *Arjuna Awards 2018:* Neeraj Chopra (Athletics), Subedar Jinson Johnson (Athletics), Hima Das (Athletics), Nelakurthi Sikki Reddy (Badminton), Subedar Satish Kumar (Boxing), Smriti Mandhana (Cricket), Shubhankar Sharma (Golf), Manpreet Singh (Hockey), Savita (Hockey), Col. Ravi Rathore (Polo), Rahi Sarnobat (Shooting), Ankur Mittal (Shooting), Shreyasi Singh (Shooting), Manika Batra (Table Tennis), G. Sathiyan (Table Tennis), Rohan Bopanna (Tennis), Sumit (Wrestling), Pooja Kadian (Wushu), Ankur Dhama (Para-Athletics) and Manoj Sarkar (Para-Badminton).
- *Dronacharya Awards 2018:* Subedar Chenanda Achaiah Kuttappa (Boxing), Vijay Sharma (Weight-lifting), A. Srinivasa Rao (Table Tennis), Sukhdev Singh Pannu (Athletics), Clarence Lobo (Hockey), Tarak Sinha (Cricket), Jiwan Kumar Sharma (Judo) and V.R. Beedu (Athletics).
- *Dhyan Chand Award:* Satyadev Prasad (Archery), Bharat Kumar Chetri (Hockey), Bobby Aloysius (Athletics) and Chougale Dadu Dattatray (Wrestling).

SAHITYA AKADEMI AWARDS

- These prizes are awarded annually to the authors of the most outstanding books of literary merit published in each of the 24 languages recognised by the Akademi.
- There are also two awards for Sanskrit and English. The award, inform of a casket containing an inscribed copper plate and a cheque of ₹ 1 lakh is given to the author or his/her heir.

DADA SAHEB PHALKE AWARD

- The award carries a cash prize of ₹ 10 lakh, a Shawl and Swarna Kamal.
- Mrs Devika Rani Roerich was the first person to receive Dadasaheb Phalke Award in 1969.
- The award for 2017 have been given to veteran actor–Vinod Khanna (Posthumously).

General Knowledge

BHARATIYA JNANPITH AWARD

- Instituted in 22nd May, 1961, carries a cash prize of ₹ 11 lakh, a citation and a bronze replica of Vagdevi (Saraswati).
- Instituted by a literary organisation in India, 54th Bhartiya Jnanpith Award, 2018 for outstanding contribution to literature, has gone to Amitav Ghosh (English).

65TH NATIONAL FILM AWARDS-2017

Regional cinema dominated the 65th National Film Awards announced on April 13, 2018. Assamese film Village Rockstars won the award in the Best Feature Film category. Baahubali 2: The Conclusion directed by S.S. Rajamouli was selected as the Best Popular Film providing wholesome entertainment. Awards in various categories are as follows:

- **Best Feature Film:** Village Rockstars (Assamese) ● **Best Director:** Jayaraj (Bhayanakam—Malayalam) ● **Best Actress:** Sridevi (Mom) ● **Best Actor:** Riddhi Sen (Nagar Kirtan) ● **Best Choreography:** Ganesh Acharya (Toilet Ek Prem Katha) ● **Special Jury Award:** Nagar Kirtan (Bengali) ● **Best Lyrics:** Muthurathinam ● **Best Music Direction:** A.R. Rahman (Kaatru Veliyidayi) ● **Best Screenplay Original:** Thondimuthalum Driksakshiyum ● **Best Screenplay Adapted:** Bhayanakam ● **Best Cinematography:** Bhayanakam ● **Best Female Playback Singer:** Sasha Tirupati (Kaatru Veliyidayi) ● **Best Male Playback Singer:** K.J. Yesudas (Poy Maranja Kalam from Viswasapoorvam Mansoor) ● **Best Children's Film:** Mhorkya ● **Best Film on Environmental Conservation:** Irada ● **Best Feature Film on National Integration:** Dhappa (Marathi) ● **Best Debut Film of Director:** Sinjar ● **Best Popular Film Providing Wholesome Entertainment:** Baahubali 2: The Conclusion.

INDIRA GANDHI AWARD FOR NATIONAL INTEGRATION

- Carnatic Vocalist T.M. Krishna was conferred the Indira Gandhi Award for National Integration for 2015-16. The award carries a citation and cash prize of ₹ 10 lakh.

SARASWATI SAMMAN

- Given for outstanding literary works, value ₹ 15 lakh. The award for 2018 has been given to Telgu poet K. Siva Reddy for his collection of poems titled 'Pakkaki Ottigilite'.

BEST PARLIAMENTARIAN AWARD

- The Best Parliament Member Award for 2015, 2016 and 2017 have been conferred on Ghulam Nabi Azad (Congress), Dinesh Trivedi (TMC) and Bhartruhari Mahtab (BJD).

KALINGA PRIZE

- This award is given each year by the UNESCO and founded by former Odisha Chief Minister late Shri Biju Patnaik for popularisation of science.

JAMNALAL BAJAJ AWARDS, 2018

- Each of the award comprises a cash prize of ₹ 10 lakh, a trophy and citation. It is given for outstanding role in different walks of life. The winners of 2018 award are Mr. Dhoom Singh Negi, Ms. Rupal Desai & Mr. Rajendra Desai, Ms. Prasanna Bhandari and Dr. Clayborne Carson.

VYAS SAMMAN-2018

- This is awarded by KK Birla Foundation for outstanding Hindi Literary work by an Indian citizen that was published in the past decade. This carries a cash prize of ₹ 4 lakh. The award for 2018 has been given to noted Telugu poet K. Siva Reddy for his Collection of poems titled 'Pakkaki Ottigilite'.

 General Knowledge

INTERNATIONAL AWARDS

NOBEL PRIZES

- These Prizes were instituted in 1901 by a Swedish scientist, Dr. Alfred Nobel; the discoverer of Dynamite.
- Six prizes are awarded annually for (i) Chemistry, (ii) Physics, (iii) Medicine, (iv) Literature, (v) Peace and (vi) Economics —started since 1969.
- The following Indians so far have been awarded these prizes: (i) Dr. Rabindra Nath Tagore (1913) for his "Geetanjali". (ii) Dr. C.V. Raman for Physics in 1930, (iii) Mother Teresa for Peace in 1979, (iv) Prof. Amartya Sen in 1998 for Economics and
  (v) Kailash Satyarthi in 2014 for Peace.

Nobel Prize 2018

- *Physics:* Arthur Ashkin (96) of USA, Gerard Mourou (74) of France and Donna Strickland (59) of Canada "for groundbreaking inventions in the field of laser physics.
- *Chemistry:* American scientists Frances H. Arnold and George P. Smith and British researcher Gregory P. Winter "for applying the principles of evolution to develop enzymes used to make everything from biofuels to medicine".
- *Physiology or Medicine:* James P. Allison of the USA and Tasuku Honjo of Japan "for game-changing discoveries about how to harness and manipulate the immune system to fight cancer".
- *Literature:* The Nobel Prize in Literature will not be handed out this year after the awarding body was hit by a sexual misconduct scandal.
- *Peace:* Denis Mukwege, a doctor who helps victims of sexual violence in the Democratic Republic of Congo, and Nadia Murad, a Yazidi rights activist in northern Iraq and survivor of sexual slavery by the Islamic State "for their efforts to end the use of sexual violence as a weapon of war and armed conflicts".
- *Economic Sciences:* US economists William Nordhaus and Paul Romer.

MAGSAYSAY AWARDS-2019

The winners of 2019 Magsaysay Award has been declared on August, 02, 2019. The 2019 awardees are:

- *Ravish Kumar (India):* Journalist Ravish Kumar, Senior Executive Editor at NDTV India, has been awarded Ramon Magsaysay Award 2019 "for harnessing journalism to give voice to the voiceless".
- *Angkhana Neelapaijit (Thailand):* She founded the Justice for Peace Foundation (JPF) in 2006. It is a network of human rights and peace advocates that documents the human rights situation in southern Thailand, providing legal assistance to victims of human rights violations.
- *Kim Jong-Ki (South Korea):* He established the Foundation for Preventing Youth Violence (FPYV) after his own son committed suicide.
- *Ko Swe Win (Myanmar):* He is the editor-in-chief of Myanmar Now, an independent online news site focused on long-form investigative pieces in both Burmese and English.
- *Raymundo Pujante Cayabyab (Phillippines):* He is a Filipino musician, composer, and conductor who is known in the industry and beyond as Mr C. He started his career in the 1970s, getting his break when his song "Kay Ganda ng Ating Musika (How Beautiful is Our Music)" won the grand prize in the first Metro Manila popular music festival in 1978.

GANDHI PEACE PRIZE

- The government instituted this ₹ 1 crore prize on the lines of the Nobel Peace Prize in 1995.

General Knowledge

- It is the highest Civilian International award by the Govt. of India. The award for 2018 have been given to Yohei Sasakawa, the goodwill ambassador of WHO.

MAN BOOKER PRIZE 2018

- Author Anna Burns has become the first Northern Irish writer, and the first woman since 2013, to win Britain's renowned Man Booker Prize for her novel Milkman.

INDIRA GANDHI PRIZE FOR PEACE, DISARMAMENT AND DEVELOPMENT

- The award was instituted in the memory of Mrs. Indira Gandhi to foster creative cooperation among nations of the world.
- The award for 2018 has been given to Delhi based environment think-tank, CSE. This prize carries ₹ 25 lakh and a citation.

OSCAR AWARD

- This prestigious award of film world is given annually by 'National Academy of Motion Picture Arts & Sciences' of America.

91st Oscar Award (Declared in 2019)

The 91st Academy Awards (Oscar) ceremony, which held on February 24, 2019 at the Dolby Theater in Los Angeles, was the first hostless Oscars in 30 years. Green Book, directed by Peter Farrelly, about a white chauffeur and his black client in segregation-era America, won best picture and two other awards. The winners are:

- **Best Picture:** Green Book
- **Best Director:** Alfonso Cuaron *(Roma)*
- **Best Actress:** Olivia Colman *(The Favourite)*
- **Best Actor:** Rami Malek *(Bohemian Rhapsody)*
- **Best Supporting Actress:** Regina King *(If Beale Street Could Talk)*
- **Best Supporting Actor:** Mahershala Ali *(Green Book)*
- **Best Foreign Language Film:** Roma *(Mexico)*
- **Best Original Screenplay:** Green Book
- **Best Adapted Screenplay:** BlacKkKlansman
- **Best Original Score:** Black Panther
- **Best Original Song:** Shallow *(A Star is Born)*
- **Best Documentary Feature:** Free Solo
- **Best Documentary Short:** Period. End of Sentence
- **Best Live Action Short:** Skin
- **Best Cinematography:** Alfonso Cuaron *(Roma)*
- **Best Costume Design:** Black Panther
- **Best Hair And Makeup:** Vice
- **Best Editing:** Bohemian Rhapsody
- **Best Animated Feature Film:** Spider-Man : Into The Spider-Verse.

MISS WORLD-2018

- This competition was established in 1951 by the 'Miss World Incorporation'.
- The winner of 2018 is Vanessa Ponce de Leon of Mexico. Nicolene Pichapa Limsnukan of Thailand was first runner-up and Maria Vasilevich of Belarus second runner up.

BAFTA AWARDS 2019

The British Academy of Film and Television Arts (Bafta) awards were handed out in London on February 10, 2019. The winners are:

- **Film:** Roma
- **Outstanding British Film:** The Favourite
- **Director:** Alfonso Cuaron, *(Roma)*
- **Original screenply:** Deborah Davis, Tony McNamara, *(The Favourite)*

 General Knowledge

* ***Leading Actor:*** Rami Malek *(Bohemian Rhapsody)*
* ***Leading Actress:*** Olivia Colman *(The Favourite)*
* ***Supporting Actor:*** Mahershala Ali *(Green Book)*
* ***Supporting Actress:*** Rachel Weisz *(The Favourite)*
* ***Orignal Music:*** Bradley Cooper, Lady Gaga, Lukas Nelson *(A Star is Born)*
* ***Cinema tography:*** Alfonso Cuaron *(Roma)*
* ***Editing:*** Hank Corwin *(Vice)*
* ***Production Design:*** Fiona Crombie, Alice Felton *(The Favourite)*.

MISS UNIVERSE-2018

* The 67th Miss Universe pageant was held on 17 December, 2018 at Bangkok, Thailand. Demi-Leigh Nel-Peters of South Africa crowned her successor Catriona Gray of the Philippines at the end of the event. Tamaryn Green of South Africa and Sthefany Gutierrez of Venezuela were adjudged the first and second runner-up respectively.

* This competition was established in year 1952 by 'Miss Universe Incorporation'.

* The winner of this competition gets 2,15,000 pounds as prize.

* The most beautiful girl is selected in this competition on the basis of her beauty and–multifarious genius.

ICC AWARDS 2018

The International Cricket Council (ICC) on January 22, 2019 named Virat Kohli the world's best Test and One Day International (ODI) player, and captain of the ICC Test and ODI teams of the year. The winners are:

* ***Cricketer of the Year, ODI Cricketer, Test Cricketer, also Named Captain of the ICC Test and ODI XIs:*** Virat Kohli (India),
* ***Emerging Cricketer:*** Rishab Pant (India),
* ***Fans Moment of the Year:*** Indian under-19 team's World Cup triumph in New Zealand,
* ***Best Umpire:*** Kumar Dharmasena (Sri Lanka),
* ***Spirit of Cricket:*** Kane Williamson (New Zealand)
* ***Associate Cricketer:*** Calum MacLeod (Scotland).

☞ Highest Honours of Some Countries

Country	Highest Honour	Country	Highest Honour
India	Bharat Ratna	Britain	Member of British Empire, Victoria Cross
Pakistan	Nishan-e-Pakistan		
Kuwait	Mubarak-Al-kabir Medal	Japan	Order of Moulovenice Sun
Saudi Arabia	Shah Abdul Aziz Medal		
Argentina	The Order of Sona Martin	Denmark	Order of Diana Brog
Nicaragua	Augusto-Caesar Sandino Order	France	Legend of Honour
		America	Presidential Medal of Freedom
Vietnam	The order of the Golden Star		
		Germany	Pore Lee Merit Iron Cross
Hungary	The Order of Banner	The Netherlands	Netherlands Lion

General Knowledge

SPORTS

OLYMPICS

- First of all these games were held by the Greeks in 776 B.C. on Mount Olympus in honour of the Greek God Zeus. In this way, the history of Olympic Games is about twenty eight hundred years old. These games continued to be held every four years until 394 A.D. When these games were stopped by a royal order of the emperor of Rome.
- The modern Olympic Games which started in Athens in 1896, are the result of the devotion and dedication of a French educator Baron Pierre de Coubertin and the first Olympic meet in the modern series was held in 1896 in Athens, the Capital of Greece. Since then, they are being held every four years except for breaks during world wars.
- The Olympic flag is white in colour with five coloured rings, each ring symbolic of a continent. Summer as well as winter Olympics are held in the same year.
- The 2020 Olympic Games scheduled to be held at Tokyo, Japan
- The official Olympic Motto is *Citius, Altius, Swifter, Higher, Stronger*. The Head Office of International Olympic Committee (IOC) is at Lausanne (Switzerland).

COMMONWEALTH GAMES

- The Commonwealth Games are held every four years, in the year in which Asian Games are held. All the Commonwealth Countries (former colonies of Britain) can take part in it.
- The first Commonwealth Games were held in 1930 at Hamilton (Canada).
- There are currently 24 members of the Commonwealth of Nations, and 71 teams participated in the games.
- The 2018 Commonwealth Games held at Gold Coast (Australia).

ASIAN GAMES

- After the Second World War, most of the Asian Countries gained independence. On the lines of Olympic Games, Asian Games were planned every four years.
- India hosted the first Asian Games in 1951.
- The 2018 Asian Games held at Jakarta (Indonesia).

WORLD CUP CRICKET

- The first Cricket World Cup was organised in England in 1975. A separate women's Cricket World Cup has been held every 4 years since 1973.

General Knowledge

124

☞ **List of Cricket World Cup**

Year	Venue	Winner/Runner
1975	England	West Indies beat Australia
1979	England	West Indies beat England
1983	England	India beat West Indies
1987	India & Pakistan	Australia beat England
1992	Australia	Pakistan beat England
1996	India, Pakistan & Sri Lanka	Sri Lanka beat Australia
1999	England	Australia beat Pakistan
2003	South Africa	Australia beat India
2007	West Indies	Australia beat Sri Lanka
2011	India, Sri Lanka, Bangladesh	India beat Sri Lanka
2015	Australia, New Zealand	Australia beat New Zealand
2019	England	England beat New Zealand
2023	India	(to be held)

HOCKEY WORLD CUP

- The first Hockey World Cup was organised in Barcelona (Spain) in 1971. Women's Hockey World Cup has been held since 1974. The 15th Hockey World Cup held in the India (Bhubaneswar) in 2018.

FOOTBALL WORLD CUP

- The Football World Cup is organised by FIFA (Federation of International Football Association). The World Cup is called 'Jules Rimet Cup' named after the name of FIFA President Jules Rimet. The first Football World Cup was organised in Uruguay in 1930.

- In 1942 and 1946, the Football World Cup was not played due to World War II.

- Brazil is the only nation to have participated in every World Cup so far. The 2022 Football World Cup scheduled to be held at Qatar.

☞ **Important Cups & Trophies**

INTERNATIONAL

✳ American Cup	: Yacht Racing	✳ Ryder Cup	: Golf
✳ Ashes	: Cricket	✳ Thomas Cup	: Badminton
✳ Davis Cup	: Lawn Tennis	✳ U. Thant Cup	: Tennis
✳ Derby	: Horse Race	✳ Walker Cup	: Golf
✳ Grand National	: Horse Streple Chase Race	✳ Wightman Cup	: Lawn Tennis
		✳ Rothman's Trophy	: Cricket
✳ Jules Rimet Trophy	: World Soccer Cup	✳ European Champions Cup	: Football
✳ King's Cup	: Air Races	✳ Grand Prix	: Table Tennis
✳ Merdeka Cup	: Football	✳ Edgbaston Cup	: Lawn Tennis
✳ Swaythling Cup	: Table Tennis (Men)	✳ Grand Prix	: Lawn Tennis

NATIONAL

✳ Agha Khan Cup	: Hockey	✳ Deodhar Trophy	: Cricket
✳ Beighton Cup	: Hockey	✳ Duleep Trophy	: Cricket
✳ Bombay Gold Cup	: Hockey	✳ Durand Cup	: Football
✳ C.K. Naydu Trophy	: Cricket	✳ Dhyan Chand Trophy	: Hockey

General Knowledge

* Dr. B.C. Roy Trophy	: Football (Junior)		* Rani Jhansi Trophy	: Cricket
* Ezra Cup	: Polo		* Ranji Trophy	: Cricket
* Guru Nanak Cup	: Hockey		* Rangaswami Cup	: Hockey
* Holkar Trophy	: Bridge		* Ramanujan Trophy	: Table Tennis
* Irani Trophy	: Cricket		* Rene Frank Trophy	: Hockey
* Indira Gold Cup	: Hockey		* Rohinton Baria Trophy	: Cricket
* Murugappa Gold Cup	: Hockey		* Rovers Cup	: Football
* Nehru Trophy	: Hockey		* Santosh Trophy	: Football
* Nixan Gold Cup	: Football		* Subroto Cup	: Football

☞ Sports Terms

* **Badminton:** Mixed doubles; Deuce; Drop; Smash; Let; Foot work; Setting.
* **Base Ball:** Pitcher; Put out, Strike; Home; Bunt.
* **Billiards:** Cue; Jigger; Pot; Break; In Baulk; In Off; Cannons.
* **Boxing:** Upper cut; Round; Punch; Bout; Knock down; Hitting below the belt; Ring.
* **Bridge:** Finesse; Dummy; Revoke; Grand Slam; Little Slam; No Trump; Rubber.
* **Chess:** Bishop, Gambit; Checkmate; Stalemate.
* **Cricket:** L.B.W. (leg before wicket); Creases, Popping-creases; Stumped; Bye; Leg-Bye; Googly; Hattrick; Maiden over; Drive; Bowling; Duck; Follow-on; No ball; Leg Break; Silly point; Cover point; Hit-wicket; Late-cut; Slip; Off-spinner; In-swing.
* **Football:** Off Side; Block; Drop-kick; Penalty-kick (or goal kick); Corner-kick; Free-kick; Dribble; Thrown-in; Foul.
* **Golf:** Boggy; Foursome; Stymic; Tee; Put; Hole; Niblic; Caddie; Links; The green; Bunker.
* **Hockey:** Carried; Short Corner; Bully; Sticks; Off side; Roll in; Striking Circle; Under-cutting; Dribble.
* **Horse racing:** Jockey; Punter.
* **Polo:** Bunker; Chukker; Mallet.
* **Tennis:** Back hand drive; Volley; Smash; Half-volley; Deuce; Service; Let; Grand Slam.

☞ Stadiums and Places Associated with Sports

Name of Stadium	Sports	Place	Name of Stadium	Sports	Place
Ferozshah Kolta Ground	Cricket	Delhi	Black Heath	Rugby Football	London
Jawaharlal Nehru Stadium	Athletics	Delhi			
Shivajee Stadium	Hockey	Delhi	Henley	Boat race	England
National Stadium	Hockey etc.	Delhi	Wimbledon	Lawn Tennis	London
Ambedkar Stadium	Football	Delhi	Wembley Stadium	Football	London
Brabourne Stadium	Cricket	Mumbai	White City	Dog-race	England
Wankhede Stadium	Cricket	Mumbai	Aintree	Horse-race	England
National Stadium	Hockey etc.	Mumbai	Tentbridge	Cricket	England
Eden Garden	Cricket	Kolkata	Patnee Martlake	Boat-race	England
Green Park Stadium	Cricket	Kanpur	Tibankham	Rugby Football	England
Keenan Stadium	Cricket	Jamshedpur			
Nehru (Chepauk) Stadium	Cricket	Chennai	Sandy Lodge	Golf	Scotland
Barabati Stadium	Cricket	Cuttack	Forest Hill	Tennis	New York
Lords, Oval, Leeds	Cricket	Britain	Brooklyn	Baseball	New York
Hedingle Manchester	Cricket	Britain	Melbourne	Cricket	Australia

 General Knowledge

☞ **Name of Playing Compound of Different Games**

Name of Compound	Related Sports	Name of Compound	Related Sports
Court	Lawn Tennis, Badminton, Netball, Hand ball, Volleyball, Squash, Kho-Kho, Kabaddi	Pool	Swimming
		Alley	Bowling
		Mat	Judo, Karate II
Diamond	Baseball	Arena	Horse Riding
Ring	Boxing, Skating, Wrestling, Circus, Riding display	Vellodrum	Cycling
		Field	Polo, Football, Hockey
		Track	Athletics
Course	Golf	Pitch	Cricket, Rugby
Board	Table Tennis	Rink	Ice Hockey

Some Important Results

TENNIS

* **Italian Open (May, 2019)**–Rafael Nadal (Spain).

* **Mandrid Open (May, 2019)**–Novak Djokovic (Serbia).

* **Australian Open 2019 (Jan., 2019)**– *Men's Singles:* Novak Djokovic (Serbia); *Women's Singles:* Naomi Osaka (Japan).

* **French Open (June 2019)**–*Men's Singles:* Rafael Nadal (Spain); *Women's Singles:* Ashleigh Barty (Australia).

* **Wimbledon (July 2019)**–*Men's Singles:* Novak Djokovic (Serbia); *Women's Singles:* Simona Halep (Romania).

* **U.S. Open (Sept. 2018)**–*Men's Singles:* Novak Djokovic (Serbia); *Women's Singles:* Naomi Osaka (Japan).

FOOTBALL

* **FIFA World Cup (July 2018, Moscow)**– France beat Croatia.

* **Santosh Trophy (April 2019, Ludhiana)**–Services defeated Punjab.

* **Super Cup (April 2019, Bhubaneswar)**– FC Goa beat Chennaian FC.

HOCKEY

* **Men's Hockey World Cup (Dec., 2018, Odisha)**–Belgium beat Netherland.

* **Champions Trophy (July, 2018)**– Australia defeated India.

* **Hockey India Junior National Championship (April-May, 2018)**–*Men's:* Punjab; *Women's:* Jharkhand.

* **Sultan Azlan Shah Hockey Tournament (March 2019, Ipoh)**–South Korea beat India.

* **National Hockey Championship (March 2018, New Delhi)**–Punjab beat Petroleum Sports Promotion Board.

BADMINTON

* **Malaysia Open (April 2019)**–Lin Dan (Men's); Tai Tzu Ying (Women's).

* **Premier Badminton League (Jan., 2019, Bengaluru)**–Bengaluru Raptors.

* **Asian Badminton Championship (April 2018, Wuhan)**–Kento Momota (Japan).

General Knowledge

* **Indonesia Open (Jan. 2019, Jakarata)**–Saina Nehwal (India).

* **Thomas Cup (May 2018, Bangkok)**–China.

* **Uber Cup (May 2018, Bangkok)**–Japan.

* **All England Badminton Championship (March 2018)**–Shi Yuqi (*Men's*), Tai Tzu Ying (*Women's*).

CRICKET

* **ICC World Cup (July 2019, London)**–England defeated New Zealand.

* **Under-19 World Cup (Feb., 2018 Mount Maunganui)**–India defeated Australia.

* **ICC Women's World Cup (July 2017, London)**–England defeated India.

* **IPL-12 (May 2019, Hyderabad)**–Mumbai Indians defeated Chennai Super Kings.

* **Ranji Trophy (Feb. 2019, Nagpur)**–Vidarbha defeated Saurashtra.

* **Irani Trophy (Feb. 2019 Nagpur)**–Vidarbha defeated Rest India.

* **Under-19 Asia Cup (Oct., 2018, Dhaka)**–India defeated Sri Lanka.

CHESS

* **Tata Steel Chess Challengers (Jan. 2018, Wijkaan Zee, Netherlands)**–Vidit Gujrathi (India).

* **Delhi GM Open (Jan. 2018)**–Arkadji Naiditsch (Azerbaijan).

* **Chennai Open (Jan. 2019)**–Levan Pantsulaia (Georgia).

* **Norway Chess Tournament (June 2019, Stavanger)**–Magnus Carlsen.

GOLF

* **China Open (May 2019)**–Mico Korhonen (Finland).

* **Augusta Masters (April 2019)**–Tiger Woods (US).

* **Thailand Open (May 2018)**–Panuphol Pittayarat.

* **Australian Open (Feb., 2018, Kooyonga)**–Jin Young Ko (South Korea)

* **Genesis Open (Feb. 2018)**–Bubba Watson.

* **Maybank Championship (Feb., 2018, Malaysia)**–Shubhankar Sharma (India)

BILLIARDS/SNOOKER

* **Asian Billiards Championship (March 2018, Myanmar)**–Pankaj Advani (India).

* **IBSF Snooker Team World Cup (March, 2018, Doha)**–India beat Pakistan.

* **World Billiards Championship (Nov., 2017, Doha)**–Pankaj Advani (India).

* **Asian Snooker Championship (July, 2019, Doha)**–Pankaj Advani (India).

9 788194 233633